D0515723

ACTIVITIES
FOR
INTEGRATING
THE
LANGUAGE ARTS

ACTIVITIES FOR INTEGRATING THE LANGUAGE ARTS

CAROL A. JENKINS
Lesley College

JOHN F. SAVAGE
Boston College

PRENTICE-HALL, INC., ENGLEWOOD CLIFFS, NEW JERSEY 07632

LB
1576
J38
1983

Library of Congress Cataloging in Publication Data

Jenkins, Carol A., 1950–
   Activities for integrating the language arts.

   Bibliography: p.
   Includes index.
   1. Language arts—Handbooks, manuals, etc.
2. Activity programs in education—Handbooks, manuals,
etc. I. Savage, John F., 1938– . II. Title.
LBI576.J38 1983   372.6′044   82–21444
ISBN 0-13-003699-4
ISBN 0-13-003681-1 (pbk.)

Editorial/production supervision and
   interior design: Virginia M. Livsey
Cover design: Marian Recio
Manufacturing buyer: Ronald Chapman
Illustrations: Susan M. Kelly

© 1983 by Prentice-Hall, Inc., Englewood Cliffs, New Jersey 07632

All rights reserved. No part of this book may be
reproduced, in any form or by any means,
without permission in writing from the publisher.

Printed in the United States of America

10 9 8 7 6 5 4 3 2 1

ISBN 0-13-003681-1 (pbk)
ISBN 0-13-003699-4

Prentice-Hall International, Inc., *London*
Prentice-Hall of Australia Pty. Limited, *Sydney*
Editora Prentice-Hall do Brasil, Ltda., *Rio de Janeiro*
Prentice-Hall Canada Inc., *Toronto*
Prentice-Hall of India Private Limited, *New Delhi*
Prentice-Hall of Japan, Inc., *Tokyo*
Prentice-Hall of Southeast Asia Pte. Ltd., *Singapore*
Whitehall Books Limited, *Wellington, New Zealand*

Dedicated to
Ted Jenkins
and
MaryJane Savage

10-26-84 gift K. Sylwester

ACKNOWLEDGMENTS

Special acknowledgment is given to Susan M. Kelly whose illustrations bring to life many of the activities found in this book.

Sincere appreciation is extended to Vinnie Simonian, Marguerite Tierney, Jeannette Richard, Cathy Procaccini and Kay Feeley for their outstanding work in the preparation and typing of the manuscript as well as for their words of encouragement.

The authors also wish to thank the Prentice-Hall staff, especially Susan Katz and Ginny Livsey whose expertise guided the production of this book.

A very special expression of gratitude is extended to Ted Jenkins for his unfailing support and understanding.

CONTENTS

LANGUAGE ACTIVITIES   141

PREFACE

Integration is a key word in teaching the language arts. While often separated for instructional purposes, the four areas of language arts—listening, speaking, reading, and writing—are integrally related in the web of communication. Children can hardly be expected to use words in speech that they can't understand when they hear them. Qualities characteristic of children's speech consistently show up in their writing. Spelling, a skill unique to written language, is largely dependent on a knowledge of speech sounds (phonics), which is also a part of learning to read. And so it goes. There is no part of language arts that is not linked to other parts.

This, then, was the prime purpose for designing and compiling the activities contained in this book: to suggest ways for teachers to promote integration of the language arts as they help children develop communication skills.

There are other purposes to the book as well. One is to directly translate theory into practice. Theory without practice is of little use in the classroom, and practice without theory is little more than an empty ritual. The activities that follow attempt to suggest ideas for teaching, along with providing a theoretical base for these ideas. In other words, there is an emphasis on the *why* as well as on the *how*.

A related purpose is to provide *updated* suggestions for teaching language arts. The past few years have brought new research and new ideas into the teaching of language arts—a greater emphasis on traditional grammar as part of the "Back to Basics" movement, a heightened emphasis on psycholinguistics, a greater emphasis on the demonstrated effectiveness of sentence combining, a renewed emphasis on the teaching of composition. Each of these trends is reflected in a practical way in the activities that follow.

Finally, a central purpose of the book is to help teachers find new and interesting ways of teaching language arts more effectively and efficiently. This book is designed as a tool and, like any tool, it will be as effective as the craftsperson who uses it. The activities are designed to help good teachers teach language arts in a more productive, and often in a more enjoyable, manner.

HOW THIS BOOK WAS WRITTEN

If this book is about integrating language arts, why is it divided into four different sections? For the same reason that curriculum and instructional programs often divide language arts—for organized treatment. Also, there are suggestions for bringing in other areas of language arts in every activity.

The four sections of the book—Listening, Speaking, Writing, and Language—reflect four broad areas of instructional foci.

Listening deals with the auditory receptive function of the language arts. But more than that, listening deals with thinking. Since listening and reading both involve the intake of information through language, a special emphasis in this section is given to the thinking skills common to both.

Speaking is an auditory expressive component. The range of activities suggested here provide a solid base for later writing activities.

Writing activities focus specifically on various components of the composition process. The activities in this section range from writing sentences to writing longer selections.

Language encompasses a variety of components of the language arts curriculum—grammar, vocabulary, parts of speech, punctuation, using the dictionary, spelling, and handwriting.

Grade-level designations are deliberately omitted from the activities. Language arts is, in many ways, an "ungraded" subject. First graders learn that sentences begin with a capital letter, but many upper grade students have yet to master this language competency. While some activities obviously lend themselves to use in the early grades (Whose Shoes Are These?) and others are more appropriate for use in the upper grades (Clues and Conclusion), most of the activities can be used with different pupils at different grade levels.

Each activity follows a carefully designed and well-structured format. After the title, a short paragraph presents the theoretical rationale or background information for the activity. Materials, when needed, are identified, although for most activities all that is needed is the language of the children. Objectives are written in instructional terms for teachers who prefer them this way and for teachers who may use these activities with children with special needs. The activity is fully described and evaluation criteria are provided. These criteria are based on the objective of each activity. Finally, suggestions are provided for extending and integrating the activity into other areas of the language arts. These suggestions can be extended much further, according to the teacher's own management of the activities.

ACTIVITIES
FOR
INTEGRATING
THE
LANGUAGE ARTS

LISTENING ACTIVITIES

How does one *teach* listening? As the medium through which we receive most of our verbal information, listening is the most basic—and perhaps most essential—component of the language arts. Most people engage in listening far more than they engage in any other aspect of language, and the pupil's ability to listen will greatly influence his or her learning both in and out of school.

Yet unlike social studies or science, listening does not have a body of information to be learned. And, unlike reading or math, it does not have a sequence of identifiable skills to be mastered. Providing instruction in listening, then, is not a cut-and-dried proposition.

Classroom instruction in listening involves providing experiences in which pupils are expected to exert conscious effort in attending to and reacting to what they hear. It includes making pupils more aware of the importance of listening in their lives. Listening occurs incidentally or informally each time a direction is given or a story is read. It occurs more directly through the types of activities suggested in this section. It can be an integral part of all oral language activities in the classroom.

Listening is more than an auditory activity. More importantly, it is a cognitive activity. "Teaching" listening is often a process of setting pupils' minds in motion while their ears are at work. Listening takes place in the mind. It extends beyond the reception of sounds to the digestion of ideas.

As a cognitive process, listening has much in common with reading. Both are receptive components of the language arts, and the goals of listening comprehension and reading comprehension are similar—and at times—identical. Pupils who can't understand a main idea, see cause-effect relationships, determine sequence, or draw conclusions based on speech can hardly be expected to perform these mental operations on what they read. With many pupils, it makes sense to develop these thinking skills through listening prior to, or along with, working on these reading comprehension skills.

Because listening is a mental activity, it is usually evaluated by monitoring pupil response to auditory stimuli, either by asking questions or by observing behavior. But listening is an active rather than a passive process. And effective listeners will send signals even as they are listening. Children can be alerted to:

- look at the listener while he/she is speaking;
- not interrupt;
- provide appropriate feedback with a nod or a point of clarification;
- ask pertinent questions about what is being said;
- not doodle or engage in other distracting mannerisms.

While none of these outward behaviors guarantees the attention or mental activity that is essential to the listening process, they are behaviors that courteous listeners practice.

Most of our daily communication takes place through the medium of speech. Effective listening instruction will help children maximize this communication.

TUNING IN

Skill Area: Listening
Attending

Background: Distractions—the clanging of the heating system, the uninvited bee, the productive but noisy creative dramatics group in the classroom corner—continuously capture the attention of young minds during the school day. Rather than just telling children to "pay attention," teachers can encourage them to explore the effect of distractions on learning. The following activity challenges children to identify factors in their classroom environment that impinge on their attending powers.

Objective: The students will tune out distracting noises and attend to the events of a story being read; they will sequence these events accordingly.

Materials: Record player; a story book; and corresponding worksheet.

Activity: Do this activity when you know there will be distractions occurring in or near the classroom; for example, another class is having recess outside your window; classes are filing back and forth to lunch. You can also plan for some distractions to occur: a small group of children can view a filmstrip in one corner of the room; a few students can be cleaning a cabinet.

As the distractions are underway, tell the class to listen to a story. Read the story without making any reference to their inattentiveness.

Pass out a worksheet (prepared in advance) with a few questions about the story. Tell the students you want to find out how well they listened.

When you notice that they are having trouble completing the assignment, ask the class to stop working, have the helpers sit down, and so forth. Remove as many distractions as possible.

Ask pupils why they had a hard time completing the worksheet and listening to the story. As distractions are mentioned, list them on the board. Ask pupils to think about distractions which bother them at other times of the day. Add these to the list. Explain that distractions are annoying and that they affect their ability to concentrate.

Have students suggest ways of reducing/eliminating some of the distracting noises. List suggestions. Discuss also the necessity of sometimes just "tuning out" the noise, pretending it is not there. As a practice activity, read another story to the class while the record player is on. Explain to students that they must tune in the story and tune out the record player. Check their listening comprehension with a worksheet asking them to put the story events in order.

Have students discuss their success in tuning out the record player. Explain that now that they know what distractions are and how they affect their listening, they should try hard to tune them out.

Evaluation Criterion: Students' ability to sequence story events after listening to a story with distractions in the background.

Extension and Integration:

LISTENING: Some children may need more practice with this auditory skill. Tape record a story or a set of directions with noise in the background. For example, tape the following set of directions while the T.V. is on as background noise: "Draw a clown. Color his hair and one button red; draw a ball in his hand." Have the students follow these directions, tuning out the distracting stimuli as much as possible.

WRITING: Have children write a paragraph about "What Bugs Me the Most" in the classroom in the way of distractions. Have them offer suggestions to overcome the distraction and share solutions with the class.

SPEAKING: Set up a buddy system in the classroom, pairing each student up with a buddy. The buddy's job is to get his or her distracted partner's attention via verbal or nonverbal cues and remind him or her to tune in.

PICTURE THIS

Skill Area: Listening
Visualization

Background: Visualization is the process of creating mental images. It is a quality essential to both listening and reading comprehension. Research (Levin, 1971; Wolff and Levin, 1972) has shown that encouraging children to create visual images results in stronger comprehension. In the following activity, children are asked to develop visual images as they listen to descriptive passages.

Objective: After listening to a descriptive passage, students will identify a picture representing the passage.

Materials: Pictures, either hand-drawn or clipped from magazines that correspond to the detailed description.

Activity: Ask students to close their eyes (or rest their heads on their desks) and imagine that a hot fudge sundae has been placed in front of them. Tell the class that the sundae has three scoops of vanilla ice cream and lots of hot fudge. Whipped cream is piled high on the sundae and the sundae is topped by two cherries.

Ask students to open their eyes. Show them three pictures: one matching the description of the sundae, the other two differing in some detail. Have the students select the picture that matches the description exactly.

Ask students to discuss how they remembered the information. Ask how many students saw the hot fudge sundae in their minds as they were listening to the description. Emphasize the value of visualizing while listening; explain how visual images will help them remember the details better. (Telling them that their mind is like a T.V. screen that can show pictures may help them catch onto the idea of imagery.) Repeat this activity with another example—a clown's face—that each student should see in his/her mind. The clown's face has a big red nose, two yellow spots on the cheek, and bright red hair that sticks out all over the head. Once again, have pupils select a picture based on the description.

Several short descriptions of this type can be used in this activity. For student response, a catalogue page containing pictures of similar objects can be used.

After practice in visualizing objects, you can dictate short action sequences and have pupils sequence the events that they visualize. Cartoon strips from the daily newspaper can be used for this sequencing activity.

Evaluation Criterion: Students' ability to select the picture that correctly represents the appropriate description.

Extension and Integration:

READING: As students read, they can be directed to identify words and phrases that create visual images in their minds.

WRITING: Students can write their own brief descriptive paragraphs and read these passages to the class. Students in the audience can draw pictures approximating their visualizations.

WRITING: For upper grade classes, pupils can take notes during oral presentations and use these notes in selecting the correct picture.

A NONSENSE STORY

Skill Area: Listening
Story Details

Background: Nonsense stories provide students with an excellent opportunity to listen attentively to identify the parts that "don't make sense."

Objective: Given a nonsense story, students will listen attentively and identify the nonsense statements.

Materials: Nonsense questions and a nonsense story (examples provided).

Activity: Have the children listen carefully to a series of questions and answer yes or no by shaking their heads accordingly:

1. Do cars overturn?
2. Do plants hibernate?
3. Do people wink?
4. Do dogs growl?
5. Do doctors evaporate?
6. Do teachers have parents?

Explain that by paying close attention to the questions, everyone was able to give the right answer. Explain that understanding what you hear is very important; if you don't understand something, you won't know what to do or say.

Tell them to listen carefully to the following football story that was written by someone who doesn't understand the game. Read the story twice; the first time read it through without interruption and ask students to count on their fingers the number of mistakes in the story; the second time ask them to raise their hands as soon as they hear an incorrect statement. Have students make corrections.

THE SUPERBOWL

It was the summer of 1983. Millions of fans arrived at the stadium to watch the big play-off between the two best football teams in the country: the Daisies and the Tulips.

As the two famous quarterbacks, DeMeo of the Daisies and Hughes of the Tulips, appeared on the field, the crowd applauded wildly.

Before the game started, each team formed a tight circle, with arms around each other's shoulders and talked about the weather. This is called a puddle. After the puddle, the game started.

The Tulips' halfback punched the ball to DeMeo, who grabbed the ball and made a dash for the touchdown line.

Hughes, who was eating a carrot for extra strength decided to try and stop DeMeo from reaching the touchdown line. He skipped as fast as he could toward DeMeo. DeMeo, who saw Hughes coming became frightened and yelled, "Here, Hughes take the ball, just leave me alone!"

Evaluation Criteria: Students' ability to listen attentively and identify nonsense statements.

Extension and Integration:

WRITING: Students can write an imaginary letter to the author of this story and explain the game of football to him.

READING/SPEAKING: Pass out a copy of the above football story to a group of students. Have them role-play the story in its nonsense form.

SPEAKING: Organize a class football game. Chances are some students won't know how to play the game. Select a group of knowledgeable players to prepare a lesson for the class and teach it.

DREAMS

Skill Area: Listening
Pre-questioning

Background: Pre-questioning—the strategy of asking questions before the material is read to the students—increases listening comprehension. Pre-questions set a purpose for the listener. In the following activity, pre-questions are posed to students before the information is presented so that students can focus their listening.

Objective: Given pre-questions, the students will listen attentively and provide the appropriate answers.

Materials: Pre-questions and corresponding passages (examples provided).

Activity: Ask, "How many of you had a dream last night?" Have students briefly share their dreams.
    Explain that in today's lesson they are going to learn more about dreams. Ask them to listen carefully to the following information so that they can answer the question, "How can you tell when someone is dreaming?" Read the following passage:

During the night when you are sound asleep and your eyes are closed, your eyeballs jump around, under your eyelids. I know that sounds hard to believe, but it is true. When your eyeballs jump around, it means you are in the stage of sleep known as REM. REM means rapid eye movement. It is during REM, that time when your eyeballs are moving, that you are having a dream.

Repeat the question, "How can you tell when someone is dreaming?" and ask students to respond. Ask students if it was easy to answer that question and have them explain why. Reinforce the idea that when a question is asked beforehand, it helps the listener focus on what is being said. Ask students to relate any other information they learned from the passage.

Read the following pre-questions and passages to students. Comment on their listening performance after each passage.

PRE-QUESTION: WHAT HAVE SCIENTISTS FOUND OUT ABOUT DREAMS?

Scientists study people dreaming in special sleep laboratories. By recording the number of times that people go into the REM stage each night, scientists were able to discover about how many dreams we have each night. They found out that everyone has four to six dreams every night. The first dream is very short and only lasts about 10 minutes. But the last dream is long; it lasts about 1 hour.

PRE-QUESTION: DO ONLY PEOPLE DREAM?

People dream. Dogs and cats dream. Horses and pigs dream. In fact, all mammals dream. Reptiles like turtles, lizards, and snakes do not dream.

PRE-QUESTION: WHAT DO PEOPLE DREAM ABOUT?

Most people dream about their family and friends. They usually dream about things they saw or did during the day. Some people dream about things they would like to do, such as riding a motorcycle.

PRE-QUESTION: WHY ARE DREAMS IMPORTANT?

Two scientists did a study to find out what would happen if people weren't allowed to dream. The scientists worked with two groups of people in their sleep laboratory. One group was allowed to sleep through the night *except* when they were dreaming. Every time their rapid eye movements started, the scientists awakened the people, then told them to go back to sleep. Therefore, the people in this group were not allowed to dream.

The people in the other group were also awakened by the scientists the same number of times, but not during their dreams. These people had their usual number of dreams.

After five days, the scientists found that people who were not allowed to dream were very nervous and fidgety during the day. They had trouble remembering things. The people in the group who were allowed to dream at night had no problems during the day.

Evaluation Criteria: Students' ability to use pre-questions to focus their listening and locate appropriate answers.

Extension and Integration:

WRITING: Encourage students to keep a dream diary. Suggest that they keep a note pad beside their bed. Explain that when they begin to wake up in the morning, they will probably be coming out of their last dream. As they wake up, they should concentrate on their dream and recall as much as possible, writing it down on the note pad. During the school day, give students an opportunity to rewrite their dreams into their diaries. Students can begin to analyze any patterns that occur in their dreams and share their findings with other students.

READING: Pre-questioning is also a valuable technique to use with children experiencing reading comprehension problems. Students can be given pre-reading questions and asked to read the passage to find the answers.

READING/WRITING: Engage students in designing pre-reading questions for other students or even the teacher. Ask students to select a piece of interesting information, read it carefully, and write one or two questions. Students can present the pre-question to the teacher/other students who will locate the answer.

USING CONTEXT CLUES

Skill Area: Listening
Context Clues

Background: Children's listening vocabularies can be strengthened through instruction in context clue usage. The following activity asks students to listen and think about the contextual material surrounding an unfamiliar word and deduce its meaning.

Objective: Using context clues, the student will arrive at the meaning of unfamiliar words.

Materials: Sentences containing nonsense words (examples provided); a story built around an unfamiliar word (example provided).

Activity: Read the following sentences which contain nonsense words to the class. Have the students use the context of each sentence to figure out what real word the nonsense word stands for:

1. The farmer was very upset when he noticed that a *flipsy* (rabbit) had hopped into his garden and eaten the lettuce.
2. The baby was hungry so her mother gave her a *bepop* (bottle) of milk.
3. "You have betrayed me and you shall be punished," cried the angry King. "Guards, take him to the *vigvat* (dungeon)."
4. Bobby pitched a ball over the batter's head and the *blapper* (umpire) shouted, "*Taz* (ball) 1."
5. The *fofer* (water) was so cold that the boys stayed on the beach and built *dop razzles* (sand castles).

Have students discuss how they knew which real words fit into the sentences. Explain that very often they can figure out the meaning of an unfamiliar word by listening carefully to the rest of the sentence.

Tell the class that they are going to listen to a story that contains a real word that they will not know. Explain that during the story they will have three chances to figure out the unfamiliar word. Each time you stop reading, ask them to write down what they think the word means.

It was Joan's twelfth birthday. She received many presents for her birthday, but the most special present was the *cereus.* Her sister had sent it all the way from Arizona. (Stop; ask students to write down what they think a *cereus* is.)

Joan looked at the beautiful *cereus.* It was green and about 5 inches long. She placed the *cereus* on the windowsill. (Stop; ask them to write down a second guess.)

Joan really didn't know how to take care of her *cereus,* so she called the florist. He told her that a *cereus* needs lots of sunshine but very little water. The spiny stalk of a *cereus* holds water for the plant. (Stop; ask students to write down their final guess.)

Students can share their range of guesses. Reemphasize the value of using context clues to figure out the meaning of unfamiliar words.

Stories using the above format can be written for each of the following unfamiliar words:

aardvark	misnomer
agama	monologue
biff	nomad
botanist	paraphernalia
chorister	rodent
croupier	seismograph

Evaluation Criterion: Students' ability to use context clues.

Extension and Integration:

READING: Basal readers frequently contain unfamiliar vocabulary words which teachers usually introduce prior to oral/silent reading. Design a reading lesson which doesn't introduce all the words in advance but which encourages students to use context clues for discovering meanings of unfamiliar words while reading.

LANGUAGE: Explain to students that reliance on context clues will often help them figure out unfamiliar words, but not always. When a word can't be deduced from context, the dictionary should be consulted. Students can be given passages in which the context does not reveal the meanings of unfamiliar words and can be asked to locate meanings in the dictionary.

WRITING: Students will enjoy searching the dictionary for a "weird" word around which a story similar to the one presented in the above activity can be written and shared with the class.

LISTENING FOR ANTONYMS

Skill Area: Listening
Antonyms

Background: Antonyms—words with opposite meanings—are typically part of vocabulary study throughout the elementary grades and beyond. Having students listen for antonyms in sentences requires attentive listening. This sort of activity is also basic to critical listening, however, since the critical listener must often listen attentively for details in what he or she hears.

Objective: Upon hearing sentences containing two words of opposite meaning, students will identify the antonyms in each sentence.

Materials: A list of antonyms that the class may be studying.

Activity: Use a list of antonyms that the class might be studying or a list that you can compose to form sentences. Each sentence should contain one set of antonyms; for example:

The *ugly* catepillar grew into a *beautiful* butterfly.
The ice cream cone turned the child's expression from a *frown* to a *smile.*

Dictate or read the sentences to the group. Students should listen carefully to identify the two antonyms in each sentence. Students can either identify the antonyms orally or they can keep a list to be checked at the end of the activity. The difficulty level of this activity can be raised by including more sophisticated words as antonyms; for example:

During his *hectic* journey, he looked for a *tranquil* place to rest.

All sentences should make sense. That is, a sentence such as "The short boy was very tall" should not be used.
Practice in context can also be developed by using one fairly easy word as part of the antonym pair and one word that is less familiar to students; for example:

I first thought the matter was *important* but I quickly realized that it was quite *trivial.*

When context is used in this way, students should identify the clues in the sentence that they used to identify the more difficult word in the antonym pair.

Students might also be asked to write sentences using antonyms in this way.

Evaluation Criterion: Students' abilities to identify the antonyms that they hear.

Extension and Integration:

WRITING: Sentence writing is a natural extension as students are asked to write their own sentences using antonyms in this way.

LANGUAGE: The same type of activity can be used for working with synonyms. Several antonyms and synonyms can be included in the same sentence and students can classify the words as the sentences are dictated.

CAN YOU FOLLOW DIRECTIONS?

Skill Area: Listening
Following Directions

Background: Throughout the school day, students are repeatedly asked to follow directions for activities of varying complexity. Successful completion of the activities often hinges on students' ability to follow directions competently. The following activity first introduces students to the steps involved in remembering directions and then asks them to follow these directions accordingly.

Objective: Given sets of directions, students will listen carefully and follow them accordingly.

Materials: Sets of directions (examples provided); string.

Activity: Ask, "Has this ever happened to you: your mother tells you to pick up your shoes in the living room and take them to your bedroom, feed your hamster, and then go and find your little brother. By the time she finishes talking, you've forgotten the first thing she said!''? Have students react. Discuss why following directions can be confusing.

Tell the students that this lesson is going to help them practice following directions. Explain that they will be able to remember the directions better if they follow these three steps:

1. Concentrate on what is being said.
2. "See" each of the directions in their minds.
3. Repeat the directions to themselves *before* doing them.

Have students implement the three steps with the following simple activity: encourage them to concentrate, see each step in their minds, and repeat the directions to themselves before carrying out the activity.

a. Stand up.
b. Shake your right foot.
c. Sit down.

Instruct them to get up and follow the directions when you say, "Do it now."

Discuss performance.

Have the class (or as a variation, divide the class into two groups; have each group take turns performing while the other group watches and gives feedback) follow the sets of directions given below. Before each set, review the steps for remembering directions. Remind them not to move until you say, "Do it now." (Move to sets containing four and five directions if children are experiencing success with simpler directions.)

a. Stand up. b. Hop around your chair three times. c. Sit down.	a. Stand up. b. Shake hands with yourself. c. Wave to the clock. d. Sit down.
a. Make a fist. b. Touch your nose, mouth, and chin with your fist. c. Fold your arms. d. Stand up.	a. Stand up. b. Bend down and touch your toes. c. Stand up again. d. Sit down.

---

a. Let your fingers walk across your desk and down the side onto your knees.

b. Put your hands in front of your face and make a funny face at them.

c. Wave to me with your thumbs.

Explain that once they have learned the steps for remembering directions, they can follow all kinds of directions. Tell class they are now ready to follow directions for organized games such as relay races.

Move to an open-space setting; divide class into teams. Review the steps for remembering directions. Remind them not to start until you say "Do it now."

RING RACE: Have each team line up, with students standing side by side. Pass out a straw to each student. Put a ring (a notebook ring, curtain ring) on the straw of the first person on each team. Instruct students to put straws in their mouths. The object of the race is to pass the ring down the line as quickly as possible. The leaders pass the rings on their straws to the straws of the persons standing beside them. (No hands are allowed during the passing.) The team to pass the ring down the fastest, wins.

Challenge students to try toothpicks and life savers.

BODY RACE: Have each student find a partner. Instruct each pair to stand side-by-side in a long line.

Give each pair a piece of string and have them tie their legs together (the right leg of one partner with the left leg of the other partner). Indicate the finish line. The first pair to reach the finish line wins.

Evaluation Criterion: Students' ability to follow oral directions.

Extension and Integration:

LISTENING: Read a set of directions to the students. Pass out a worksheet with the same directions in jumbled order. Have students put the directions in order.

READING: Numerous activities which require children to read and follow directions can be designed, for example, how to make arts and crafts projects, how to do a science experiment, how to play a game.

WRITING: Have students create their own relay races. The directions can be written down and read to the class by the authors. Students can follow directions accordingly.

DIRECTIONS FOR SCHOOL ASSIGNMENTS

Skill Area: Listening
Following Directions

Background: In providing instruction in following directions, it is important to help students make the transition from fun-related activities (directions for playing a game) to school-related activities (directions for a math assignment). In the following activity, students practice following directions for school assignments.

Objective: The students will listen to sets of school-related directions and follow them accordingly.

Materials: Sets of directions (examples provided).

Activity: Give an example of a recent activity for which you had to repeat the directions a number of times. Discuss this frustration with students. Review their performance in the previous activity, "Can You Follow Directions?" (pp. 13–15).

Suggest that following directions for games is very similar to following directions for assignments—both require the student to remember the directions and follow through.

Review the steps for remembering directions and ask students to try them out on the following mini-assignments:

---

a. Take this piece of paper and write your name at the top.

b. Copy the message on the blackboard (I can follow directions).

c. When you are finished turn your paper over.

d. Do it, NOW!

Discuss their ability to recall and follow this set of directions.

Repeat this procedure with the following mini-assignments. After each set of directions has been carried out, comment on performance.

---

a. Take out your math book.

b. Open to page 23.

c. On the back of your handwriting paper, do problem #1.

> d. Put your book away.
>
> e. Do it, NOW!

Pass out paper.

> a. Fold your paper in half like this (demonstrate) so that you have two long columns.
>
> b. Write the words Loud Noises in the first column and Soft Noises in the second column.
>
> c. Look at the list of words on the board. Write the words that make loud noises in the Loud Noise column. Write the words that make soft noises in the Soft Noise column.
>
> d. Do it NOW!
>
> *Word List:* bee, mouse, truck, whisper, cannon, hammer.

Pass out paper.

> a. Take out your reading books.
>
> b. Use the table of contents to find a poem in your book.
>
> c. Read the poem.
>
> d. On the paper, write the name of the poem and its author.
>
> e. Draw a picture of what the poem is about.
>
> f. Do it NOW!

Evaluation Criteria: Students' ability to follow directions.

Extension and Integration:

LISTENING: Students will not master the skill of following directions in one or two lessons. They will need repeated reinforcement and practice in following directions. Encourage them to attend carefully when daily assignments are being given and compliment them as frequently as possible (a chart which stars those activities in which the whole class/group followed directions well may be beneficial).

SPEAKING: Have students brainstorm as many situations as possible in which they are asked to follow directions and identify who the direction-giver is, for example:

baseball field—coach
dentist's office—dentist

READING: Rather than always giving oral directions, write messages on the board for students to read and follow, for example:

> Time for Lunch. Clear off your desks.
> Sit quietly so I know you are ready.

EYEWITNESS

Skill Area: Listening
Sequencing

Background: Sequencing is an important component of the listening process, requiring students to recall story events in the order in which they occur. Since sequencing places heavy demand on a student's memory, initial instruction in this skill should allow students to rely on both auditory and visual input. The following activity asks students to sequence events that have been received both visually and auditorily.

Objective: The students will observe a skit and identify the sequence of major events.

Materials: A skit (example provided).

Activity: Ask if anyone has ever been an eyewitness to an accident or a crime. Have students relate incidents and explain the term "eyewitness." Stress the importance of witnesses being able to tell the events they observed in exactly the right order.

Tell the students to watch the following skit carefully and as eyewitnesses keep track of the story events.

Have two students who have already rehearsed the following skit, act it out for the class.

SETTING: CLASSROOM
TIME: 12 NOON
CHARACTERS: JOAN, PAT

   PAT: *(Walking to Joan's desk)* Joan, can I borrow your scissors? I have one more shape to cut out before lunch.

> JOAN: (Washing her desk top) Sure, you can use them, just remember to put them back. I'm going to rinse off this sponge. (Before going to rinse off the sponge, Joan puts her lunch money on the left-hand corner of her desk top. While she is at the sink, the teacher walks by Joan's desk, notices the money, and places it inside her desk.)
>
> (Meanwhile, Pat returns Joan's scissors.)
>
> JOAN: (Looking on her desk for her lunch money) Hey, where's my money? Somebody stole my money! Pat! Pat! Where's my money?
>
> PAT: (Running over to Joan) What's wrong?
>
> JOAN: (Shouting) Did you take my money?
>
> PAT: (Upset) No! I just returned your scissors. Where was the money?
>
> JOAN: (Pointing) Right here. I'm telling the teacher.

Ask students in the audience to raise their hands if they know what happened. Before letting anyone respond, instruct students to order the events of the story in their mind (or on paper). Have students then report the sequence. List events on the board. Discuss their performance as eyewitnesses and the role of sequencing in reporting.

Evaluation Criteria: Students' ability to use auditory and visual information and recall the sequence of major events.

Extension and Integration:

LISTENING: Students can watch films of the award-winning Caldecott stories, using the auditory and visual information presented to recall the sequence of each story's events.

SPEAKING: Students can discuss the moral dilemma presented in the above skit. Students can share experiences in which they have been unjustly accused of wrongdoing and identify possible solutions.

SPEAKING: Crises of varying intensity occur every day in the school setting. Students can sharpen their observation skills and describe the sequence of events that took place.

POLICE REPORT

Skill Area: Listening
Sequencing

Background: The previous activity introduced students to the concept of sequencing by asking them to order events of information received visually and auditorily. In the following activity the visual input is removed and students are asked to listen to a story and recall its sequence of events.

Objective: The students will listen to a story and write the sequence of major events.

Materials: Story (example provided); police report worksheet (example provided).

Activity: Ask the students to imagine what it would be like to overhear two criminals talking about a crime they had committed. Ask students what they would do and why. Emphasize the importance of relating events of the crime in sequential order.

Have students listen to the following imaginary event and concentrate on the story's sequence.

You are at the playground one afternoon sitting inside a cement tunnel. You suddenly hear two people talking. They must be leaning against the tunnel. You listen.

A man's voice says, "I'm out of breath. I can't run any further."

"We can take a break here," a woman's voice replies. "The police will never think to look for us in a playground."

The voices stop. You freeze. You can't believe your ears. You realize that they don't know you are in the tunnel.

"Where's the diamond?" asks the man.

"Right here in the secret panel of my shoe," says the woman.

"Everything went off as planned," says the man. "I got to Norton's Jewelry Store at 9:05 just as Mr. Norton was opening the diamond case. I walked into the middle of the room and pretended to faint. Mr. Norton came running over, loosened my tie, and opened my shirt. He didn't even see you slip in the side door."

"Well, I am short," the woman replies. "I was able to duck behind the counter, slip my hand into the case, and grab the diamond. I was out of there before Norton finished helping you onto your feet."

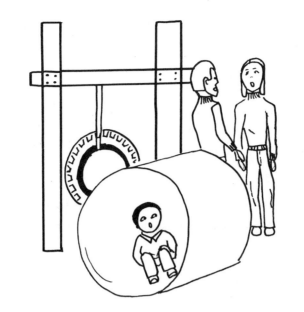

"Now, if we can only make it to the train station," the man says. "Come on."

You remain very still. After a few minutes you peek around the tunnel to make sure the coast is clear. Then you race to the police station. The police officer asks you to fill out a Police Report (pass out Police Report worksheet), instructing you to write down everything the robbers said in the exact order that they said it.

POLICE REPORT

Name: _____

Address: _____

Telephone: _____

Description of Suspects: _____

_____

_____

Where you saw suspects: _____

_____

_____

Time: _____

Describe what you saw or heard in the order in which it occurred: _____

_____

_____

_____

_____

Have students read their reports and compare their sequences.

Evaluation Criteria: Students' ability to listen and recall story events in order.

Extension and Integration:

WRITING: Ask students to pretend that instead of going to the police with the story, they decide to follow the robbers. Have them write about the sequence of events that follow in the get-away adventure.

SPEAKING: Students will enjoy dramatizing the crime scene described in the above activity because it is full of action.

READING: Select a number of comic strips in which the sequence of events is evident, making sure that the reading level is appropriate to your students. Glue a picture onto the back of each comic strip, then cut up and scramble the frames. Have students read each frame and sequence them accordingly. Students can self-correct their work by flipping over each frame in its place; if the picture is in order, the frames were properly sequenced.

TWO OF A KIND

Skill Area: Listening
Categorizing

Background: Whenever auditory input occurs beyond the "hearing" level, thinking is necessarily part of the activity. This listening/thinking activity is based on students' ability to see relationships as well as to listen attentively. It is adaptable to both formal and informal settings.

Objective: Given three words or expressions, students will be able to tell which two belong together and will be able to justify their choices.

Materials: None.

Activity: Ask students to listen attentively as you say three words. Tell them that you want them to pick out the "two of a kind," that is, the two words that belong together. Students must also tell why they made the choice they did. Identifying the criterion for pairing two of the words or expressions together should be considered more important than getting the "right" answers.

Items for this activity can be selected on the basis of:

SOUND ELEMENTS: (Different answers can be justified using different criteria)

book	wagon	*balloon*	(initial sounds)
cat	*mat*	tree	(rhyming words)
worm	*ladder*	*rabbit*	(number of syllables)

OBJECT CLASS:

dog	*truck*	*car*	(both classes of vehicles)
carrot	apple	*turnip*	(both vegetables)

SEMANTIC MEANING:

sad	*depressed*	joyful	(similar meaning)
smiling	*pleasant*	painful	(similar connotation)

OTHER MEANING ASSOCIATIONS:

French	*Russian*	Swedish	(both have salad dressings named after them)

Categories for making associations are all but limitless. Giving reasons for making the associations should be stressed.

A leader can ask pupils items in turn; or once pupils are used to the idea, each pupil can make up and ask the next item when he or she has answered correctly.

Evaluation Criteria: Students' abilities to make and defend their choices.

Extension and Integration:

SPEAKING: Students working in pairs or small groups can make up additional items for later use. Pupils can construct items from words and concepts from different content areas of the curricula.

SPEAKING: Students can discuss in small groups reasons why different associations are appropriate.

YOUR FIRST PUPPY

Skill Area: Listening
Main Ideas and Details

Background: Main ideas and details enhance listening comprehension by providing students with a framework for organizing the incoming auditory information. Students recall details with greater ease when they are attached to a unifying idea. The following activity provides students with an opportunity to listen to factual information and identify the main ideas and details.

Objective: Given factual passages, the student will identify the main ideas and supporting details.

Materials: Factual passages (examples provided).

Activity: Ask students to listen carefully to the following four words and identify the one that describes the others: poodle, collie, dogs, terrier. When students respond, illustrate the words as follows:

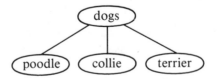

Ask students to explain the diagram. Introduce the term *main idea* in reference to the big circle and the term *detail* in reference to the small circles. Explain that the details talk about the main idea.

Have the students listen to the following series of words and identify the word that gives the main idea:

1. cherry, fruit, peach, apple
2. bee, butterfly, ant, insect
3. man, girl, people, woman
4. ball, puzzles, toys, dolls
5. money, quarter, nickel, dime

Explain that thus far they have been listening for the main idea of single words; now they will listen to some passages and figure out the main idea.

Ask students to listen and identify what the following story is about:

> When you go to the pet store to buy a puppy, you want to be sure to buy a healthy one. Check its coat of fur; it should be thick and look shiny. Look at the puppy's eyes and ears to make sure they are not runny. Smell the puppy; it should smell clean.

Ask the students to state what the passage was about; illustrate the main idea accordingly. Ask students to relate some of the details and complete the diagram:

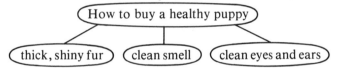

Reexplain that the main idea tells what the passage is about; the details talk about the main idea. Point to each detail and show how it ties into the main idea.

If students respond to the original question (what is the main idea?) with an incorrect answer such as "Puppies shouldn't have runny eyes," they are confusing important details with the main idea. At this point, it would be beneficial to reread the passage and ask the students to see if the whole passage is about "Puppies shouldn't have runny eyes." Redirect their attention to the general idea of the passage.

Read the following passages and have students listen and identify the main ideas and supporting details.

> If you are taking your puppy home by car, you need to be prepared. Bring a roll of paper towels because your puppy will probably get carsick. It's also a good idea to bring a cardboard box with paper lining the bottom. Your puppy will probably be frightened by the moving car and may not stay in your arms. Placing it in the box will make it feel more secure.

For the first few days, your puppy will show signs of being homesick for its family. It will whine and cry a lot, especially at night. It may go to the bathroom often and may even have diarrhea.

What can you do to help your puppy sleep through the first few nights? You can add a pillow to its bed to make it more comfortable. You can wrap a hot water bottle (not too hot) in a towel and place it in the puppy's bed to make it warm. You can also try another idea: wrap a ticking clock in a towel and place it in the puppy's bed. The puppy will think that its mother is close by and will remain calmer.

Evaluation Criteria: Students' ability to listen to factual material and identify main ideas and supporting details.

Extension and Integration:

READING: Find a paragraph that contains a main idea and details. Write each sentence on a separate strip of paper. Scramble the sentences and have the students locate the sentence that contains the main idea and place it on top; students can then arrange the remaining details. Students can also be given paragraphs in which they circle the main idea.

SPEAKING: Children love to talk about their puppies/dogs or other pets. Encourage children to discuss other aspects of pet care such as feeding, bathing, grooming.

WRITING: Give students some pictures from magazines and have them create titles for each picture. To write a title, students must be able to identify the main idea of the picture.

RADIO NEWS

Skill Area: Listening
Details

Background: Before the advent of television, which provides simultaneous auditory and visual stimuli, people had to depend entirely on their listening skills for a large part of their information and entertainment. The following activity is designed to recapture attention to auditory stimuli as a means of acquiring and retaining information.

Objective: Having heard a series of news items, students will recall the items in detail.

Materials: None required, although a radio might be used to extend the activity.

Activity: Prepare a "Classroom News Report." This report can focus on items of class, school, or local news of immediate interest to the pupils. Or items can be extended to current events, with items of state, regional, national, or international scope. Initially, news reports shouldn't contain any more than five stories. The amount of elaborate detail can vary according to the level of the class, but each item should contain at least the essential *who, what, when, where, why,* and *how* of the story. The stories can be taken from the local newspaper, or from a classroom newspaper such as *My Weekly Reader.*

Read the news report to the entire class. Students will be expected to listen attentively to remember what the stories were and to retain all the details they can about each story. Students can be questioned individually on what they remembered, or they can be grouped to make lists of everything they heard in the report. Students can also be asked to read their local newspapers to bring in clippings for use in the News Reports. For practice in oral reporting, pupils can take turns "broadcasting" daily reports to the classroom.

Near the end of the school week, a large "Week In Review" report can be planned by the students. This might consist of the most significant stories "broadcast" during the week.

As an extension, the class might listen to a real radio news broadcast for the same purpose.

Evaluation Criterion: Students' ability to recall items in the news reports.

Extension and Integration:

WRITING: Have students write their own items to be included in these Radio News Broadcasts.

READING: Reading skills are involved in having students locate items to be included in the report. As students read the report to the class, purposeful oral reading is involved.

WRITING: Students can be asked to take notes on the news reports. A blank outline sheet with columns headed *Who, What, When, Where, Why,* and *How* might be included to help pupils structure their notes. The results of these note sheets might be used for rewriting continuing stories.

WHOSE SHOES ARE THESE?

Skill Area: Listening
Drawing Conclusions

Background: The act of drawing conclusions is a critical listening skill which demands a high level of thinking. To draw a conclusion, students must go one step beyond what is explicitly stated and figure out what has occurred. The following activity asks children to listen to short vignettes and, using visual aids (shoes), draw appropriate conclusions.

Objective: The students will listen to short vignettes and draw conclusions about the kind of shoes the character is wearing.

Materials: Assortment of shoes; short vignettes (examples provided).

Activity: Find some magazine pictures of people wearing different shoes. Cut the shoes off. Tape the people to the board. Scramble the shoes and also tape them to the board.

Have students examine the pictures and match shoes with appropriate pictures. For example, point to a picture of a man in his bathrobe opening a refrigerator door in a dark kitchen. Ask students what kind of shoes he would be wearing. Challenge them: "Could he be wearing sneakers?" It's possible, but not probable; have them explain why.

After the shoe match-up, bring out a box that contains the following actual shoes (sneakers, sandals, clogs, ballet shoes, children's tie shoes, slippers). Place each pair on the table in front of the class. Also place a number on each pair of shoes.

Instruct the students to listen carefully to the following short stories and figure out which shoes the person in each story is wearing. To illustrate, read the following story and have students identify the appropriate shoes by writing the corresponding number on a piece of paper.

> "What a great game! When Ed hits that ball, I'm going to run as hard as I can to get a home run."

Have students share the number they chose and why. Ask what kind of game is being played; how do they know? Compliment them on doing a good job at listening carefully. Explain that often when they listen to stories or conversations, the story doesn't tell exactly what happened but if they think hard, they can figure it out and draw a conclusion.

Tell them to listen carefully and draw conclusions about the shoes the following characters are wearing. Instruct them to write the number of the shoes on their paper.

> "Jack, it's pouring rain outside. Change your shoes or your feet will get soaking wet because they are not covered," said Jack's mother. (sandals)

> "Katie, please take off your shoes. The baby has just fallen asleep and I'm afraid those shoes will make too much noise." (clogs)

> Vinnie finished tying her new shoes. As she walked across the floor, she slipped and fell down. (leather tie-shoes)

> "Stretch, higher, higher. Keep those legs straight. Now stand on your toes and twirl around," said the teacher. (ballet shoes)

Evaluation Criterion: Students' ability to draw conclusions.

Extension and Integration:

SPEAKING: Students can bring in a pair of their favorite shoes for Show & Tell. Students can describe their shoes, explain why they like them, and share an experience they had while wearing these shoes.

WRITING: Hand out large pieces of construction paper. Have students fold the paper into six boxes. In each box, have students draw a pair of their shoes. Under each picture, they can write a description of the shoes and an explanation of when they wear them.

CLUES AND
CONCLUSIONS

Skill Area: Listening
Drawing Conclusions

Background: Rather than short vignettes, the following activity provides children with an opportunity to listen to a lengthy, more complex episode and draw a conclusion from the story clues. Students must offer evidence to support their conclusions.

Objective: The students will listen to events of a story and write a conclusion along with supporting clues.

Materials: Story (provided).

Activity: Ask, "What does a detective do?" (Solve crimes.) "How?" (Clues.) "What does he do with the clues?" Discuss responses with the students. Then ask them to listen carefully to the clues in the first part of the following story and see if they can figure out what happened.

"Hey, Dad, don't forget about my baseball game," said Katie gulping down her glass of orange juice. "Today's the big playoff."

"Wouldn't miss the game for anything," said her father, closing his leather briefcase. "What time does it start?"

"Six o'clock on the button," said Katie.

"OK. I've got to run or I'll miss the bus," he said, fixing his tie in front of the mirror.

"Oh, Dad, when are we getting a new car? I hate taking the bus," Katie complained.

"As soon as I get enough money," he called and ran out the door.

Later that afternoon at the ball park, Katie was ready to pitch the first inning of the big game. She looked around for her dad, but saw no sign of him. She wound up and fired the first pitch of the game.

"Ball one," called the umpire, and so went the entire afternoon with more walks than earned runs and a very embarrassing loss.

On the bus ride home Katie's thoughts were not on the game but on her dad: "He promised he'd be there. How could he have let me down like this?"

As she got out of the bus, she heard a car horn beeping. "Katie, over here." It was her father in a brand new car. "Hey, Katie, sorry I missed the game. I had something to do," said her father hurriedly.

"But, you promised . . . ," started Katie.

"I know. Forgive me. How do you like our new car?" smiled her father.

"Where did you get the money?" asked Katie.

Her dad laughed, "Oh, I found a pot of gold. Now, no more questions. Hop in. I'm taking you to buy that new bike you wanted."

The next morning Katie was listening to the news and heard the following report: "Last night at about 6:30, a robber broke into the bank and stole over $30,000. An eyewitness spotted the man, dressed in a suit and carrying a ripped leather briefcase, as he dashed out of the bank."

Katie's father walked into the kitchen and picked up his briefcase. Alarmed, Katie said, "Dad, your briefcase is torn."

"Oh, I must have ripped it on the bus yesterday. I'm in a hurry, dear. Have a good day," said her father.

Pass out a worksheet with the following diagram:

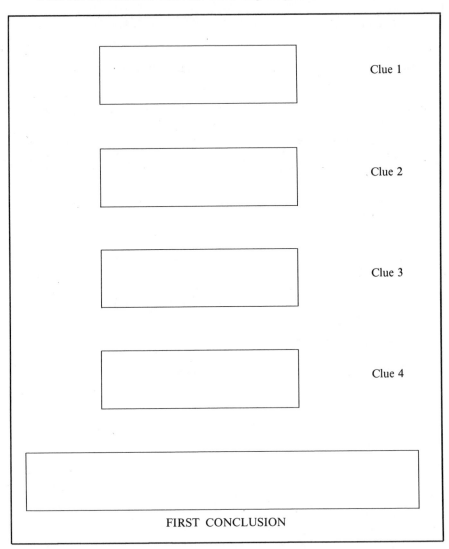

Direct students to the large rectangle at the bottom of the worksheet marked conclusion and say, "If you were Katie, what would you conclude?" Have students write their conclusions in the large rectangle. Direct students to the clue boxes. Have them write in the major clues that lead to their conclusion.

Discuss students' clues and conclusions. Emphasize the relationship between clues and conclusions. Once the skill of drawing conclusions is grasped, students can discuss the moral dilemma facing Katie. Ask if Katie has accumulated enough solid evidence to verify her conclusion. Ask students what they would do under similiar circumstances. Explain that sometimes listeners can only draw tentative conclusions about a situation and must search for further clues.

Read the remainder of the story to the class.

As Katie was getting ready for school, she heard her mother arriving home from work. Katie raced downstairs.

"Hi, Katie," smiled her mother as she gave her a hug. "Where is your father? I hope I haven't missed him already."

"You did. He left for work about ten minutes ago. Mom, I have to tell you something . . . ." blurted Katie.

"Oh, no!" interrupted her mother. "I wanted to surprise him with this new briefcase."

"Why?" asked Katie wringing her hands.

"Well, before I went to work at the hospital last night, I met Dad at the car dealer's to take a test drive in the new car we were buying. Dad had his briefcase on the front seat and as I moved it to the back seat I accidently caught it on the door frame. It ripped. I didn't tell him about it because I wanted to surprise him with a new one. I thought it would be a nice way to congratulate him on his big bonus." smiled her mother.

"What bonus?" asked Katie.

"You look so surprised. Didn't Dad tell you that he sold the most computers for his company and earned a big bonus?" said her mother. "You should be very proud of him!"

"Oh, I am!" shouted Katie, feeling very relieved.

Pass out a worksheet similar to the one presented above which has clue boxes and a large rectangle labelled FINAL CONCLUSION. Have students now draw a new conclusion about Katie's father and why he didn't watch her ballgame. Discuss results.

Evaluation Criterion: Students' ability to draw a conclusion supported by clues.

Extension and Integration:

LISTENING: Students can match wits with Encyclopedia Brown and attempt to solve baffling cases. Donald Sobol, author of the *Encyclopedia Brown* books, provides students with excellent practice in drawing conclusions.

READING: Student will enjoy playing *Clue,* a commercial game that challenges players to figure out who committed the crime. Stories in basal readers also provide students with opportunities to draw conclusions about characters and story events.

WRITING: After the students have listened to the first part of the story and have completed the first worksheet, have them write a story about Katie's search for further clues concerning her dad and the robbery.

MAKE A PREDICTION

Skill Area: Listening
Predicting Outcomes

Background: The following activity is a direct adaptation of Russell Stauffer's D-R-T-A (Directed Reading-Thinking Activity). In his book, *Directing the Reading-Thinking Process,* Stauffer (1975) presents an instructional strategy for actively involving students in the reading process. Students are required to think critically about what they are reading, make predictions about the story, and read to confirm or reject their predictions. Since the listening process and the reading process parallel each other so closely, Stauffer's strategy can easily be adapted to the listening process.

Objective: The students will listen to parts of *The Giving Tree* and make predictions about the story events.

Materials: Shel Silverstein's *The Giving Tree* (1964).

Activity: In order to illustrate the directed listening-thinking activity, Shel Silverstein's *The Giving Tree* has been selected.

Read the title, *The Giving Tree,* to the class and have them examine the picture on the front cover. Ask "What do you think the story is about?" As students offer predictions, encourage them to expand on their ideas. Ask the students to ponder what else a tree could give, aside from apples.

Ask students to listen carefully to the first section of the story to find out whether their predictions were right. Read only the first stage of the tree-boy relationship, the boy's childhood. At that point, stop and ask the children to explain any of their predictions that were confirmed. Reread the sentences that confirm their predictions.

Continue reading the next part of the boy's life (adolescence) as far as the boy's request to the tree for money. Ask the students to predict what the tree will do to help the boy. Read the remainder of that section. Have students discuss their predictions.

Continue reading about the boy's manhood as far as the boy's request to the tree for a warm house. Ask students to predict the outcome; read the remainder of that section and have students confirm their predictions.

Ask students to predict the next stage of the boy's life and what he will request of the tree. Finish the story and allow students to confirm their predictions.

Evaluation Criteria: Students' ability to listen and make predictions about a story.

Extension and Integration:

LISTENING: After the story, ask inferential comprehension questions to gauge the students' ability to think critically: How do you know the tree loved the boy? How would you describe the boy? Do you think the boy loves the tree? Do you know any people who are like the tree? the boy? If you were the tree would you stop loving the boy?

READING: For a detailed account of D-R-T-A, consult: Stauffer, Russell. *Directing the Reading-Thinking Process.* New York: Harper & Row, 1975. Using D-R-T-A in conjunction with the students' basal readers can bring new life and energy to reading lessons.

LISTENING/WRITING: Select another story and read half of it to the class. Encourage students to write the story's ending and compare their predictions with the author's ending.

THAT'S A FACT (OR IS IT?)

Skill Area: Listening
Fact and Opinion

Background: People are bombarded every day with waves of information that they are expected to process through listening. While pupils can't be expected to recall each detail presented to them, they do need to listen carefully to determine the accuracy of what they hear. The following activity is designed to engage students in attentive listening and keen thinking.

Objective: Given a series of spoken sentences, students will distinguish those that are factual from those that are not.

Materials: A list of "Fact" and "Nonfact" statements.

Activity: Write the word *FACT* on the chalkboard and have pupils suggest definitions for it. Help students understand that a fact is something that is certainly and strictly true. A fact is a piece of information that can be proven to be true.

Use students' own experiences to illustrate facts that are true and those that are not; for example:

The school served pizza for lunch yesterday. (Assuming this is true)

The school served beans for lunch yesterday. (Assuming that the lunch was pizza)

Have pupils suggest ways of proving a fact.

Read a list of sentences containing information—some true and some not true—to the class. Have students identify those that are facts and those that are not facts. Statements can be drawn from their own experience:

An egg yoke is white.

Thanksgiving comes in April every year.

Or, statements can be drawn from social studies or other areas of the curriculum:

Columbus discovered America in 1942.

An aphid weighs 100 pounds.

6 times 7 is 44.

Students should listen attentively to each statement and respond accordingly.

As a related lesson, write the words *FACT* and *OPINION* on the chalkboard. Explain that the difference between these two terms is that a fact can be proven to be true, while an opinion is a belief that is not always provable. Show the difference between the two types of statements.

FACTS	OPINIONS
Pizza is a nutritious food.	Pizza is the most delicious food in the world.
America has begun to explore outer space.	We should spend more money exploring outer space.

Read a series of fact and opinion statements to the class and have pupils listen carefully to indicate what each statement is. The statements can be on matters of national policy, local issues, school concerns, or personal experiences.

As a means of involving all students more intensively, have each student make a pair of cards, one with the letter "F" for Fact and one with the letter "N" for Not a fact (or the letter "O" for Opinion). As each statement is read, have students hold up the appropriate card. This response technique requires a response from each student to each statement and it lets the teacher know which students are answering in which way.

Evaluation Criterion: Students' ability to identify factual statements.

Extension and Integration:

WRITING: Have students write their own series of Fact/Nonfact statements to share with others. This can be done as review of content area materials, or students can practice research skills in locating information for their statements.

READING: The ability to distinguish fact from opinion is an important critical reading skill. Help pupils identify the fact/opinion differences in material that they read in the classroom or at home.

SPEAKING: Have students discuss some of the Fact/Opinion statements used in the activity. Students tend to accept certain opinion statements as facts; for example, "This nation is the best in the world." Have pupils discuss both sides of a popular opinion statement that most or all accept as fact.

SEX ROLES ON TV

Skill Area: Listening
Recognizing Stereotypes

Background: Listening involves more than hearing. It involves thinking, and often observation as well. The following activity is designed to engage children's minds, as well as their eyes and ears, as they watch television.

Objective: Students will recognize sexist stereotyping that they observe on television.

Materials: None.

Activity: Although this activity is designed to be done by pupils as they watch television at home, preparation in the classroom is important.

Discuss with the class the role of television in their lives, how important it is to them, how much time they spend watching it, what they learn from T.V. Take a vote on the students' favorite show.

List the main characters from the show and discuss what their characters are like in terms of their looks, their interests, their personalities, their occupations, their concerns or "conflicts" in the show. Discuss the differences that are apparent between males and females in the shows.

Ask students to identify two or three commercials that involve humans. (Many of the commercials shown during children's programming involve cartoon characters rather than humans.) Once again, discuss the differences between males and females in the commercials. Questions such as the following can be used to focus discussion: What do the women on the commercials do? The men? What kind of products do women advertise? What products do men advertise? What types of men and women *don't* ever appear on commercials?

As children watch television at home, ask them to keep a record for a day or a week on the differences they observe between the way males and females are portrayed on television. An observation checklist, based on questions raised in class, can be prepared for use at home. The results of this observation can be discussed in the classroom.

Evaluation Criterion: Students' completed observations.

Extension and Integration:

WRITING: In the upper grades, students can write a formal essay, based on their observations, on the roles of males and females as they are portrayed on television.

SPEAKING: Students can discuss or debate whether or not men and women are stereotyped on television.

READING: Students can be alerted to look for sex role stereotyping in books, magazines, and newspapers that they read.

THE READING GROUP

Skill Area: Listening
Details/Main Idea/
Predicting Outcomes

Background: Reading aloud in groups is a common practice in most elementary classrooms. When asked why they engage in this "round robin" reading practice, most teachers say that one of their purposes is to improve their students' listening skills. If listening skills are to be improved in these instructional settings, adjustments need to be made.

Objective: After listening to other students read in a reading group, the student will retell the substance of the story and/or respond correctly to questions based on the story.

Materials: Basal readers or other reading materials used in reading groups.

Activity: Follow normal procedures for a directed reading lesson as explained in basal manual. When one pupil is asked to read aloud, *ask other pupils to close their books and listen to the reading.* Having them not follow along a line of print with their eyes is important. The focus should be on listening to other pupils in the group.

Ask questions based on the material read. The questions might be taken from the basal manual or they can be teacher-designed. The questions should include a variety of literal, inferential, and critical response questions and can be geared to the range of specific comprehension components normally included in reading instruction (main idea, cause-effect relationships, sequence, predicting outcomes, and so forth) Occasionally, the pupil who is reading can be the one who asks the questions.

Using oral reading as a specific focus for listening skills has another particular advantage. By its nature, oral reading is far slower than silent reading. As one student reads aloud and other students in the group follow the lines of print that the reader is reading, the other students' eyes are necessarily moving slowly. By only listening and not following the print with their eyes, there is less danger of being conditioned to slower reading.

Evaluation Criterion: Students' ability to answer questions based on the reading.

Extension and Integration:

READING: Because the activity is conducted in direct conjunction with reading lessons, reading is necessarily involved.

SPEAKING: For each story, the teacher (or one of the students in the group) can formulate and ask a discussion question based on material read or based on one of the pupil's responses.

I AM A DISABLED PERSON

Skill Area: Listening
Emotional Response

Background: The following letter was penned by a disabled person. This letter, which recounts some vivid childhood experiences, was written to help sensitize children to some of the concerns and feelings of disabled persons. Students are asked to listen and think critically about issues of primary importance to the disabled.

Objective: The students will listen critically to a letter written by a disabled person and react orally and in writing to issues addressed in the letter.

Materials: The letter (provided).

Activity: The following letter is written in two parts. Tell the class that in part one Maureen talks about architectural barriers; ask if anyone knows what an architectural barrier is; explain the term. Ask them to listen to the letter and be able to tell why these architectural barriers are such a problem.

PART ONE:

Dear World,

Yesterday, we had a fire drill in school. I was working by myself in the library when the alarm went off. I walked as quickly as I could to the front door. A couple of kids in front of me opened the door and rushed out. By the time I got to the door it had closed shut. I tried with all my might to open it but couldn't. It was just too big and heavy for a small person like me. I panicked and thought, "I could be trapped in here." Luckily a janitor saw me and let me follow him outside. Just another close call; next time I might not be so lucky!

You see, I am a physically handicapped person. I have a rare bone disease that has stunted my growth. I am about as tall as your four-year-old brother or sister—not very tall for a sixth grader. Because of my condition, I have a hard time moving around. I used to wear a brace to help straighten my right leg but I don't anymore.

So now you can see why I panicked that day. Big heavy doors are a problem for disabled people. They are just one example of the architectural barriers with which disabled people have to deal. Telephones are another example. I can't make a phone call anytime I want to because the

---

telephones are too high for me to reach. I usually have to wait until somebody comes along and is willing to dial a number for me. Doesn't seem fair, does it?

Then there's the girl's room with all kinds of architectural barriers. The toilets, sinks, mirrors, and paper towel dispensers are often too high to reach. I always carry Wash and Dries with me and hope that my hair doesn't need combing!

For a handicapped person, getting on and off buses is like jumping hurdles. The first step is just too high for short people and on many of the old buses, there isn't even a railing to hold on to.

Luckily things are beginning to change because the government passed a law that requires public buildings to eliminate architectural barriers. That means that changes have to be made in buildings to make it easier for disabled people to get around. For example, each building should have a ramp so that people in wheelchairs can get in; and telephones should be lowered so that disabled people can reach them.

Explore the issue of architectural barriers with the class. The following questions can be used to guide the discussion.

1. Are architectural barriers a serious problem for disabled people—in some cases a matter of life and death?
2. Have you ever encountered an architectural barrier? Explain.
3. How do you feel about the law that eliminates these barriers from public buildings? Will these changes in buildings cause a problem for nondisabled people; for example, will a nondisabled person be able to use a telephone that has been lowered?
4. What about private buildings—they aren't required to make any changes? Do you think they should?

After the discussion, have the students (working in pairs) write a short letter to you about the following issue:

Pretend that Maureen is a member of this class. We are very concerned about what happened to her during the last fire drill. What plans should we make for the next fire drill to ensure her safety?

PART TWO:

Buildings are not the only things that need changing, though. People's attitudes about the disabled also need to be changed. Let me give you an example: a few weeks ago I told the guidance counselor that I wanted to be a veterinarian. When he heard this, he laughed a little and said, "Oh I don't think that is a good idea.

You are too small. A big dog could knock you over." I was very upset about this. I love animals and want to work with them. I told my teacher what he said, and she made me feel much better. She said "Most horses are bigger than people, yet veterinarians examine and operate on them. So I'm sure you could find a way to work on big dogs. In addition, there are many branches of veterinary medicine. You need to explore these branches and see which one interests you the most."

This is the same teacher who helped me talk to the kids on the softball team. The first day that I went to join the team, some of the kids said there was no way that I could play. I wouldn't run fast enough and I wouldn't be able to hit the ball. My teacher listened to them and asked if they had ever heard of Debbie Phillips. Nobody had.

My teacher told them Debbie Phillips was a champion skier and a champion jockey—two pretty great achievements for a girl who was born with only half of a right leg! Debbie's right leg only goes to her knee and yet she has done incredible things in sports. The other kids were amazed. At that point, I told the team that while I couldn't run fast or bat a ball, I was a good catcher. After a brief demonstration, the kids let me join the team. Some kids still give me a hard time, but other kids think I do a good job.

It sure is great to have a teacher who understands and accepts me for what I am. She doesn't feel sorry for me or say "poor dear" like some people do. I hate that, because then people treat me like I'm a hopeless human being and I'm not. I have feelings and dreams and things I want to accomplish just like nondisabled people. Anyway, the world sure would be a nicer place to live if there were more people like my teacher around!

Your friend,

Maureen

Discuss the following issues with the class:

1. Do you think the guidance counselor meant to hurt Maureen's feelings by telling her she couldn't be a veterinarian?
2. Why does Maureen like her teacher so much?
3. Why do people feel sorry for handicapped people? Should they?
4. Have you ever talked to a handicapped person about his or her handicap? Why is it important to find out about a handicapped person's feelings?
5. Have you ever seen anyone make fun of a disabled person? Tell what happened. Why do people do this? How do you feel about it?

Ask students to write a response to the following situation:

Pretend a group of your friends are going roller skating. Ruthie says "Let's invite Maureen to go." "I don't think that's a good idea," says Jane. "She probably can't skate. Let's not ask her."

Evaluation Criteria: Students' ability to listen critically and respond orally and in writing to the letter.

Extension and Integration:

WRITING: Today, Maureen Brennan is a graduate student at Boston University's School of Social Work. She wrote this letter with hopes of helping children better understand the issues that face disabled people. She invites your students to write to her about any of the issues concerning the disabled. Students can mail their letters to:

Ms. Maureen Brennan
21 Greenwood Avenue
Hyde Park, MA 02136

SPEAKING: Encourage children to share experiences they have had with disabled people. Direct the discussion to disabled children in the school. Have students generate ways of involving their disabled peers in more school activities.

WRITING: Have students examine their school building for architectural barriers. Letters can be written to the superintendent alerting him or her to the school's noncompliance with the law.

SPEAKING: Ask students to examine magazine ads to discover how frequently disabled persons appear in advertisements. In addition, ask students to identify commercials on T.V. in which products are sold by disabled persons. Discuss findings. Have students speculate on the reasons for the virtual nonexistence of disabled persons in the advertising world.

LAST DAY OF SCHOOL

Skill Area: Listening
Emotional Response

Background: This activity is as much for you as it is for your students. Teachers often say that from year to year each class seems to have a personality of its own—a uniqueness directly attributed to the individuals making up that class. The creation of the *I Will Remember You* book is a tribute to those individuals with whom you have shared the last school year.

Objective: The student will listen to and acknowledge a personal memory from the *I will Remember You book*.

Materials: *I Will Remember You* book (example provided).

Activity: The creation of the *I Will Remember You* book will be most successful if the writing is done over a period of time. Start with your class list and as you scan the names, jot down incidents/memories that come to mind immediately for certain students. Continue to add to the list over the next few days until a memory can be associated with each student.

To make the booklet, you will need four or five ditto masters. Divide each master into four or six sections and write an entry for each student. Be sure each entry accents the positive. Draw a line across the bottom of each entry so that students can fill in the person's name. Here is a sample entry:

Remember the day you brought in that little bottle with stones in it and asked us to guess where the stones came from? We guessed your back-yard, the beach, a special collection, but we weren't right. When you told us that they were your mother's gallstones, we nearly flipped!

_____

Lead into the *I Will Remember You* book by asking students to think back over the school year and identify experiences/incidents that they will always remember. Have students share these personal thoughts.

Share your special feelings about the school year and students. Introduce the *I Will Remember You* book. Pass out the booklet to each student. Ask students to listen/read along as you share the first entry; in addition ask the person whom the entry is about to stand up at the end of the reading. Everyone can write his or her name on the blank line and contribute anything they remember about the incident.

Interest in the book will probably be high enough to complete the activity in one sitting, although a small number of entries could be presented at different times during the day.

Tell the class that you plan to save this book for many years so that you can remember all of them.

Evaluation Criteria: Students' ability to listen critically and identify a past memory.

Extension and Integration:

WRITING: Reverse roles and let the students write an *I Will Remember You, Teacher* book. Each student can write about an important memory he or she has about you. The memories can be compiled, bound into a book, and shared with the class.

SPEAKING: Students, in small groups, can discuss other good memories they have of each other, as well as of the teacher.

READING: Encourage students to take their books home and read the entries of students known to their parents, who can try to guess each mystery person.

SPEAKING
ACTIVITIES

Over the past several years, the study of psycholinguistics has generated a great deal of interest in, and a great deal of information about, the process of language acquisition. While this study has produced conflicting theories about how children acquire language, it has also produced one overriding conclusion; that is, barring severe physical or mental handicap, children acquire language long before they enter a classroom for the first time. They come to school largely equipped with language that meets their daily communications needs.

The function of oral language activities in the classroom, then, is to keep this oral language development moving apace, to help children expand and refine their skills in oral communication. This involves helping them learn to choose the word that best expresses an idea. It includes practice in the amenities of small group interpersonal communication. It entails the development of poise and self-confidence in speaking before large groups. It encompasses the ability to use speech as a vehicle to express one's thoughts clearly, accurately, and effectively.

Speech is the foundation of competency in dealing with print, both in reading and writing. As a child encounters a word in reading, the meaning of the word will be clear only if it is part of the child's listening/speaking vocabulary. Similarly, comprehending what is read often depends on understanding the grammatical relationships inherent in spoken language.

Speech is no less important as a basis for competency in writing. It's unrealistic to expect a pupil to write any better than he or she can speak. Writing ability, especially in the upper grades, depends on vocabulary size, the organization of thoughts, the use of standard language forms—all qualities that contribute to effective speech as well.

Effective oral language is marked by a pupil's ability to:

- participate willingly in formal and informal classroom activities;
- choose words to convey ideas clearly;
- speak loudly and clearly enough to be heard by others;
- use modulation through variations in pitch, stress, and juncture;
- speak without "cluttering" ideas with the repetition of such expressions as "ah," "m-m-m-m," "OK," "like," and other common distractors;
- listen to the language of other speakers in groups and respond appropriately to the language of others.

(These standards may be adapted to a checklist that might be used to evaluate classroom oral language activities. Additional items may be added according to the nature of the activity and according to the teacher's purpose in planning it. For example, "sticking to a single topic" would be an appropriate standard for evaluating discussion.)

The activities suggested in the following pages, combined with the many spontaneous occasions that arise for speech during the normal school day, will provide for a range of speaking and thinking skills appropriate to effective oral communication.

DAY ONE

Skill Area: Speaking
Interviewing

Background: The first day at school offers an opportunity to engage students in a closely integrated language arts experience, one that involves the four language arts areas of listening, speaking, reading, and writing.

Objective: Each pupil will introduce one classmate to the entire class and write at least a three-sentence biography of that classmate.

Materials: None.

Activity: Divide the class into pairs. Match pupils who are not well-known to one another. In other words, try to keep best friends, neighbors, or children from the same classroom last year apart, if possible. Have pairs of pupils interview one another. To structure the interview, the teacher might suggest a list of sample questions: most exciting thing done; most interesting or unique fact that can be said about the child; list of favorites (movies, books, TV shows, colors, foods, etc.). Children can suggest other questions, but they should be reminded that interviews should accentuate the positive. Suggested questions may be listed on the chalkboard. As pupils interview one another, they should take notes. Speaking from the notes, at a later time during the first day, each child should introduce his or her partner to the whole class. Using interview notes, each child should write a brief (depending on the age, grade level, and ability level of the group) biography of his or her partner. Contents of these biographies should be based solely on the content of interview notes. As an exercise in proofreading, each child should read the biography written about him or her before the writing is passed to the teacher. These biographies, perhaps accompanied by photographs, can be used as an effective "Meet Our Class" bulletin board display at the beginning of the year.

Evaluation Criteria: Children's effectiveness in speaking before the class in introducing classmates; production of brief written biographies.

Extension and Integration:

READING: Have children write biographies *before* introductions are made to the whole class. Place the biographies in a box. Each pupil draws a biography from the box and reads the introduction to the class.

Handwriting: Have pupils recopy the biographies prior to the writing's being used for the "Meet Our Class" display. Explain the importance of using good handwriting that other people can read. The display can be placed on the outside of the classroom door.

Writing: On the basis of information collected through interviews, have pupils write a "class poem" with a line or two for each person in the class.

CLASS HOST/HOSTESS

Skill Area: Speaking
Announcements

Background: Poise and confidence in speaking before a group are important aims of large-group oral language activities. But poise and confidence develop only with practice. Opportunities for formal oral reporting do not occur enough in the normal classroom routine to provide enough practice for the development of these important speaking qualities. This activity provides opportunities for "mini oral reports" all week long.

Objective: Given the necessary information, students will orally report this information to the class with poise and confidence.

Materials: None.

Activity: When assigning "jobs" to the class, appoint one student class host/hostess for the week. Set up a special desk closest to the classroom door for the weekly host(ess). The job of this student is to greet and introduce visitors to the class and to make all announcements that are delivered by messengers to the classroom.

Some preparation for this assignment will be necessary. Pupils should be instructed in interview techniques to determine the nature and purpose of the guest's visit to the classroom. Questions of the guest should be limited to two or three. The host(ess) should be instructed to introduce him/herself and to tell why he or she has been assigned to greet each guest.

Before reading announcements that have been delivered via classroom messenger, the host(ess) should be taught to read the message silently before attempting to read it aloud to the class. Appropriate volume, expression, and other speech qualities should also be emphasized.

The assignment of host(ess) should be made on a rotating basis so that all pupils can have the opportunity to engage in the regular large-group speaking exercise that the assignment produced.

Evaluation Criterion: Students' poise and confidence in reporting the information to the class.

Extension and Integration:

LISTENING: This activity necessarily involves both individual listening skills (as the student interviews visitors to the classroom) and group listening skills (as the class listens to the host or hostess presenting the information).

SPEAKING: This activity also provides opportunities for instruction and practice in interviewing, as the host(ess) is responsible for interviewing visitors to the classroom. Instruction in this skill should include attention to how to open an interview, how to phrase questions, and how to practice the social amenities of speech.

WRITING: The class host(ess) can also be responsibile for keeping records of number of class visitors per week, number of students ordering hot lunches, forms to be returned from home, and the like.

COMMUNICATION GAME

Skill Area: Speaking
Giving Directions

Background: Effective listening and speaking skills are two primary goals of language arts instruction. The following activity (or variations of it) has been used to heighten people's awareness of the importance of communication in business, industry, the military, and education.

Objective: The students will demonstrate effective oral communication skills by giving and following directions accurately.

Materials: Design sheets.

Activity: Prepare several sheets with easily reproducible designs; for example:

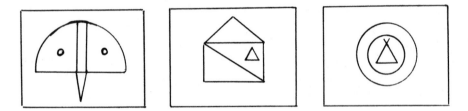

Choose one student as the speaker and have the speaker give directions to the class on how to reproduce the design. Emphasize the importance of giving and following directions carefully and accurately. After the activity, have students check their designs against the original design sheets.

This activity can be done in a variety of ways. For example, instead of having one student give directions to the whole class, pairs of students can be seated back-to-back and each can take turns giving directions. As another variation, the speaker can stand behind a screen so that the listeners can't see his or her facial expressions or body movements while he or she gives the directions. To make the activity easier, the listeners may be allowed to ask question.

As students become more adapt at this activity, more intricate designs can be used.

As a follow-up, students can use a brief check list to evaluate the speakers' directions; for example:

Did the speaker speak loudly enough?   Yes No
Did the speaker speak too quickly?   Yes No

Did the speaker repeat him/herself too often?   Yes   No

Did the speaker use words that we could easily understand?   Yes   No

Additional items can be added according to the needs and level of the class. The results can be discussed following the activity.

Evaluation Criterion: The accuracy of the reproduced designs.

Extension and Integration:

WRITING: Have students make up their own designs and write directions for others to follow.

SPEAKING: Do the activity in conjunction with another area of the curriculum; for example, constructing a bar graph in math, conducting an experiment in science, or making and following a map in social studies.

SPEAKING: Plan a discussion following the activity on why accuracy in speaking and listening is important. Have students list situations where such accuracy would be especially important.

FIRST DAY AT A NEW SCHOOL

Skill Area: Speaking
Brainstorming

Background: Transferring to a new school can be an anxiety-producing situation for most children. Having students discuss this topic and having them brainstorm ways of making a new pupil welcome can be rewarding for both parties. Brainstorming is an effective problem-solving technique that fosters creative thinking.

Objective: Pupils will brainstorm and record at least ten ways of making a new student welcome in school.

Materials: None.

Activity: Ask pupils what they think it might be like to transfer to a new school. Discuss their responses. Ask pupils who may have had this experience to share their thoughts with the class. Ask the class to suggest one or two things they could do to make a new student feel welcome in your classroom. List their initial responses on the board.

Divide the class into groups of three to five pupils each. Write the word *BRAINSTORM* on the board and explain that you want each group to brainstorm, to think of as many ideas as they can of making a new student welcome in the school. Review the *Rules of Brainstorming* with the class:

- You have five minutes to think of as many ideas as you can; the more, the better.
- Choose a recorder to write down ideas; the recorder writes as fast as he/she can, not worrying about spelling while jotting down ideas.
- All ideas are welcome; none are considered "too silly" to be written down.
- Everyone has a chance to talk; nobody criticizes another person's ideas.

The teacher should move from group to group to stimulate discussion when ideas lag. At the end of 5 minutes, have the recorder in each group read the list of group responses that he or she has recorded. Ask each group to decide on which two suggestions are most practical. Have the recorders read their groups' suggestions to the entire class. Have a "class secretary" record these ideas on the board.

Evaluation Criteria: The quantity and quality of ideas suggested.

Extension and Integration:

SPEAKING: In a large group setting, discuss relative value of the ideas suggested. Allow pupils who have transferred to a new school to direct the discussion. Group members can then agree on the two best ideas and implement them.

WRITING: Have pupils write real or imaginary letters to a new class-mate, making the child welcome in a new school.

WRITING: As a class project, have the group prepare a School/Neighborhood/Town Guide for New Students. Pupils should research interesting aspects of the history of the area, points of interest, a "Who's Who" section, and so forth.

HAMSTER CASTLES

Skill Area: Speaking
Discussion

Background: The following activity engages children in "task talk" which, according to Moffett and Wagner (1976), is the "incidental talk" that "arises naturally as a by-product of doing other things." The creation of the

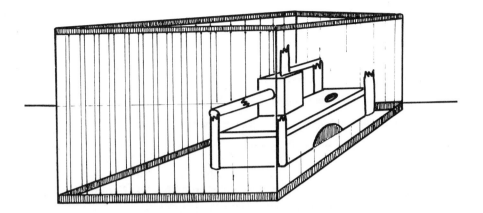

hamster castle necessitates spontaneous communication among group members. The focus of the activity is on the communication process not the product.

Objective: The students will discuss the creation of a hamster castle with other group members and present the completed products to the class.

Materials: Cardboard boxes and rings, scissors, paste, tape.

Activity: Ask "How many of you have seen the hamster mazes that are sold in stores?" Show a picture, if possible, or give a description; discuss purpose.

Suggest that since store-bought mazes are very expensive, students can create their own mazes out of cardboard boxes. The mazes can even be made in the shape of a castle.

Identify the one major drawback to cardboard mazes: they're not transparent. Have students in groups brainstorm ways of getting around this problem (such as, cut out lots of holes so hamster can peek through; place pieces of food in open areas; build castle turrets for hamster to climb out on, and so forth). Review the brainstorming process; stress that negative comments interfere with group progress. Once each group has identified some good solutions to the drawback, they will be ready to start.

Have each group discuss the task of creating a hamster castle and decide how various jobs will be completed (for example, who will measure the hamster cage; who will examine castles in library books; who will cut and paste boxes). Stress the importance of group cooperation and communication.

Each group can present its hamster castle to the class and explain its solution to the problem.

Each member of the group can then respond to the following questionnaire:

---

1. How did the group decide who was going to do different jobs?

2. Did you like the job you got?

3. Did you have a chance to give your idea?

4. Did anyone throw out your ideas or make fun of you?

5. What would make your group work even better next time?

Collect questionnaire and compile results. Present the results to the class for further discussion. Ask students to come up with some Group Talk Rules that everyone will try to abide by for the next group task.

NOTE: The problem of having five hamster castles for one cage can be resolved by either saving the castles as replacements for the ones the hamster will chew up or offering castles to other classrooms which have hamsters.

Evaluation Criterion: Students' ability to communicate effectively during group project.

Extension and Integration:

READING: Have students learn more about their classroom pet by reading books on hamsters. Have students read about gadgets that are often found in hamster cages and encourage them to make homemade versions.

WRITING: Since a number of classrooms in the school will probably have hamster cages, students can write the directions on how to make a hamster castle so that other students can construct them for their classrooms.

LANGUAGE/VOCABULARY: Have students investigate the official name of various parts of a castle and use this new vocabulary in their presentations.

AMUSEMENT PARK 2000

Skill Area: Speaking
Discussion

Background: Predicting the future or guessing what life will be like decades from now is fascinating for adults and children alike. Bringing discussions of this topic into the classroom fosters futuristic and creative thinking and provides an exciting vehicle for the development of oral language skills.

Objective: Students will create and describe an amusement park that might exist in the twenty-first century.

Materials: Assorted "building" materials such as cardboard boxes, string, small blocks of wood, wire, pipe cleaners, bottle caps, etc.

Activity: Have students recall their experiences at amusement parks or carnivals. Encourage students to tell about their favorite rides, games, attractions, foods. Encourage students to use specific language that will recreate the sights, sounds, smells, tastes, and feelings of their experiences. Ask the class what they think amusement parks will be like in the twenty-first century. Have them think about increased speeds, greater thrills, or other features that will characterize their futuristic amusement park.

Divide the class into groups of four or five pupils each, and ask each group to brainstorm for a few minutes about what rides might be available in the twenty-first century. Encourage them to be creative and to include as many details as possible for their new ride. As group members suggest ideas, one pupil should sketch the ideas.

Using the "building materials," have each group construct its futuristic ride. Then, each group will plan an oral presentation describing the ride to the rest of the class and "selling" their ride to potential customers. Presentations should include such details as size, how long the ride takes, speed, type of motion, safety features, and so forth. Each group should make its presentation to the class.

All the rides can be assembled into one area for a "Class Carnival 2000."

Evaluation Criteria: Students' creative thinking in creating their "rides" and their effective application of speaking skills as they describe their rides to the class.

Extension and Integration

WRITING: The class can prepare a brochure describing their new amusement park and convincing people to visit the park. As a prewriting activity for upper grade classes, techniques of persuasive writing and propaganda might be reviewed. Brochures on real amusement parks might be examined.

WRITING: The students' creations easily lend themselves to an imaginative writing experience, with story starters like, "I'll never forget the day Amusement Park 2000 opened!" or "As the Whizzo started moving, I knew we were in trouble."

SPEAKING: Other classes might be invited to visit the Amusement Park 2000 so that individual pupils may take turns describing the project to large groups of visitors.

HOW REAL ARE
BASAL READERS?

Skill Area: Speaking
Discussion

Background: For a long time, basal readers have been criticized for their content. Many basal stories, particularly in the early grades, are said to portray "cardboard characters" engaging in shallow, pleasant experiences. The following activity engages pupils in critical thinking by having them discuss differences between their own real lives and the events and characters portrayed in basal stories.

Objective: Through discussion, students will list differences between events of their own lives and the events in the lives of characters portrayed in basal stories.

Materials: None.

Activity: Divide the class into discussion groups of three or five students each. Remind students of the basic ground rules for effective discussion; that is, only one person speaks at a time, members are courteous to one another, the discussion stays on the topic.

Have each group recall a basal story they have recently read, one that is "reality based" rather than fantasy or folklore. Have pupils list the characters in the story they choose and think of three or four words to describe each character. Make sure that students can defend what they say about the character with events from the story. In other words, warn them that if they call a character "stupid," they must tell what that character did that led to that descriptive word.

Ask students to apply a "Reality Score"—perhaps on a scale of 1 to 10—to the characters and to the story. As a means of applying this score, have students judge the likelihood of this person really existing and/or the likelihood of this story really happening.

When students are finished discussing this topic in small groups, have groups share their results with the class; pupils who discussed the same stories can compare specific results.

Evaluation Criteria: Students' ability to judge a story's "reality" and students' ability to use effective discussion skills.

Extension and Integration:

READING: This activity, by its very nature, extends to reading by making pupils more critical readers as they read basal stories. This discussion may, in fact, be carried on effectively in a reading group after pupils have read a particular story.

WRITING: Pupils might rewrite the basal story with a great touch of reality.

BIKE SAFETY

Skill Area: Speaking
Discussion

Background: One of the keys to a successful group discussion is an engaging topic—a topic which stimulates student interest. For most children, bike-riding is an enjoyable sport as well as a major source of transportation; yet few are knowledgeable on the subject of bike safety. The following activity helps children explore this subject through discussions.

Objective: Given a copy of the rules of the road, the student will discuss the details of an accident and identify the party at fault.

Materials: If possible, copies of road regulations from the state or local Department of Motor Vehicles; toy cars and toy bikes.

Activity: Ask the students to raise their hands if they ride a bike. Ask students to raise their hands if they have been in a cycling accident or have witnessed one occur.

Explain that each day three or four students will have an opportunity to share their experiences (possibility: declare it Bike Safety Week). Explain that the purpose of this sharing is to try and figure out why so many cycling accidents occur each year and what can be done about it.

Give students time to prepare their reports which should include:

a. the setting;
b. where the vehicles were before the accident;
c. objective details of the accident;
d. the outcome.

To facilitate their presentations, students can recreate the accident scenes. A street intersection can be drawn on the blackboard and students can be supplied with toy cars and bikes.

Remind speakers to know their material well and to use appropriate volume and pace.

Divide the audience into groups and instruct them to pay close attention so they can ask appropriate questions about the accident. After the question and answer period, each group will discuss the accident and decide who was at fault and why.

1. A bicycle is a vehicle. Cyclist must obey the same rules as motorists.

2. Ride with the traffic, not against it.

3. Keep to the right side of the road

4. Obey all traffic signals, stop at red lights, stop signs.

5. Give hand signals when you are making a turn.

6. When you are making a left, stop the bike and walk it across the intersection at the crosswalk.

Groups can then share their decisions. Inevitably, questions concerning the rules of the road will arise. Present the above chart to the class; or pass out copies of rules and regulations to students, obtained from your local Department of Motor Vehicles.

Have the groups discuss the rules of the road as they apply to each student's accident report. Hang the chart on the wall as a daily reminder of bike safety.

Evaluation Criteria: Students' ability to discuss details of accidents and arrive at appropriate conclusions.

Extension and Integration:

WRITING: Students interested in cycling as a hobby can write to one of the following bicycle organizations to obtain information about local cycling activities, low-cost bicycle trips, and amateur cycling competitions:

Amateur Bicycle League of America
137 Brunswick Road
Cedar Grove, NY 07009
American Youth Hostels, Inc.
National Campus
Delaplane, VA 22025

READING: Bike safety encompasses far more than knowledge of rules of the road. Students can read cycling books to find out about buying a bike, bike maintenance, road hazards, and so forth. Suggested: Sullivan, George. *Better bicycling for boys and girls.* New York: Dodd, Mead, 1974.

SPEAKING: Have students plan a series of activities for Bike Day as a way of sharing their newly acquired information with other classrooms—especially younger children. Students could chalk in road intersections in the playground and demonstrate rules of road to the younger audience.

IF YOU WANT
MY ADVICE

Skill Area: Speaking
Problem Solving

Background: The Dear Abby column of a newspaper holds an attraction for most readers—perhaps because the letters often mirror their own problems or because a curiosity about other people's troubles takes hold. In the following activity students are asked to discuss a Dear Abby letter and propose, through group consensus, a solution for the problem.

Objective: The students will react to a Dear Abby letter and propose a viable solution to the problem.

Materials: Dear Abby letter.

Activity: Ask if anyone has ever heard of or read the Dear Abby column of a newspaper. Discuss responses. Explain that a columnist is a writer who gives advice to people who write in about their problems.

Ask students if they have ever given advice to anyone. Have students share experiences. Ask students to identify the qualities that a person giving advice should possess, such as: be a good listener, see both sides of the issue, make suggestions based on their experiences. List student responses on the board.

Tell students they will have an opportunity to be advice-givers. Read a Dear Abby letter—preferably from a child—to the class. Divide the class into small groups and ask students to discuss the problem identified in the letter. Encourage each group to focus their discussion as follows:

1. Restate the problem so that everyone has a clear understanding.
2. Relate any experiences that approximate those of the writer.
3. Explore both sides of the issue explained in the letter.

After the discussions, review the steps to brainstorming (presented in earlier activity, First Day At A New School, p. 51) and have each group then brainstorm possible solutions. Have students review these solutions and arrive at a consensus as to the best possible solution. Have groups share their advice and the rationale for it. Encourage students to challenge the advice of other groups through questions, examples, and so forth.

Read Dear Abby's advice to the writer. Discuss similarities/differences between her advice and theirs. Discuss the reasons for differences.

Evaluation Criterion: Students' ability to propose a solution to the problem.

Extension and Integration:

WRITING: Review letter-writing procedures with students. Encourage them to write a letter to a local columnist, asking advice about problems that may be troubling them. Mail the letters and hope for results. Students, of course, could write anonymous letters about personal problems which could be responded to by the teacher and/or the class.

READING/SPEAKING: Select Dear Abby letters for students to read and have them react to Abby's advice.

SPEAKING/READING: Have students explore the various roles that advisors have in our society (such as, Presidential Advisor, financial advisor, psychologist, college advisor,) and what their qualifications are. Students can research Dear Abby's qualifications and compare results.

FOLLOW THE YELLOW BRICK ROAD

Skill Area: Speaking
Movement (Creative Dramatics)

Background: Creative dramatics is one of the best ways to prepare children for more formal speaking activities such as show-and-tell and oral reporting. Immersing children in creative dramatics serves not only to enhance communication skills but also to build self-confidence. This is the first in a series of creative dramatic activities. Free movement, the first stage in creative dramatics, encourages children to let their imaginations guide their body movements. Since everyone is moving freely at the same time, inhibitions evaporate. Through body movements alone, the characters in The Wizard of Oz come alive.

Objective: The students will move like the characters in The Wizard of Oz.

Materials: Wizard of Oz scenes (examples provided).

Activity: Ask "How many have watched The Wizard of Oz on TV?" If a number of students are unfamiliar with the movie, read the story version to them.

Tell students to watch carefully as you act out one of the characters from The Wizard of Oz. To convey the meanness of the Wicked Witch of the West:

a. turn your head quickly from side-to-side and scowl at the class;
b. point your finger at them, with all fingers extended and tense;
c. toss your head back and give a wicked laugh.

As soon as students identify the character, ask what clues helped them figure out who it was. Have students ride around the room on a broom as the Wicked Witch of the West. Discuss how body movements convey meaning.

Present the following scenes from The Wizard of Oz; have students think about each character and freely move around the room as a whole group, pretending to be that character. As a variation, the class could be divided into two sections, each section taking turns to perform while others observe and comment. For added effect, play music from the movie.

Remember when Dorothy found the scarecrow in the cornfield and helped him down from the stake. How did the scarecrow move? How would the scarecrow skip? Bend?

Dorothy and the Scarecrow found the Tinman in the forest, but his body had rusted so badly that he couldn't move. When Dorothy oiled his body, the Tinman moved in a funny way. Can you walk like the Tinman? Run? Hop?

Lion was hiding in the forest and tried to scare Dorothy, Scarecrow, and Tinman. How does a ferocious lion move? Roar?

Everyone soon found out that Lion wasn't ferocious, he was cowardly. How did the cowardly Lion move? Roar?

After each performance, discuss the variety of movements.

Students can then be divided into groups of four, each student taking one role: Dorothy, Scarecrow, Tinman, Lion. Have students pretend that the yellow brick road stretches around the classroom. The four students, arm in arm, move as their character would as they:

a. walk along the yellow brick road;
b. skip along the yellow brick road;
c. walk drowsily through the field of poppies;
d. sneak into the witch's castle;
e. walk tremblingly down the corridor to meet the Wizard of Oz.

Comment on variety of movements.

Evaluation Criterion: Students' ability to express meaning through body movement.

Extension and Integration:

LISTENING: No course in creative dramatics would be complete without students moving to the music and directions of Hap Palmer, and Miss Nelson and Bruce, whose records can be loaned from most local libraries.

SPEAKING: Students in groups can act out minor characters in The Wizard of Oz and have the audience guess the characters by their movements (flying monkeys, munchkins, Good Witch of the East, Toto).

WRITING: Lion requested courage from the Wizard, Tinman a heart, Scarecrow a brain. But the Wizard couldn't give these precious gifts. Have students write a letter to their favorite Oz character and explain how one finds courage or a heart.

SHOW YOUR FEELINGS

Skill Area: Speaking
Pantomime (Creative Dramatics)

Background: Pantomime, the next rung on the creative dramatics ladder, "is the art of conveying ideas without words" (McCaslin, 1980, p. 51). Children are encouraged to use body language to convey meaning to the audience. The following activity focuses on the expression of feelings through body motion.

Objective: The students will pantomime given situations to convey appropriate emotions.

Materials: Mime cards (examples provided); a full-length mirror.

Activity: Stand at the front of the room with your arms raised in a cheer and a big smile on your face (have some good news ready). Students will quickly ask what's happened. Before answering, ask why they think something happened? Discuss the body movements and facial expression. Stress that without using any words, we often send messages through our body movements.

Ask the students to walk in a circle and let their bodies convey a feeling of sadness, fear, joy, and so forth. Discuss a variety of ways to show each feeling.

Divide the class into small groups. Have one group sit at a table on which a full-length mirror has been arranged to rest sideways. Attach a pocket to the mirror containing emotions cards:

One student is to close his or her eyes and pull out a card. The other students read the emotion, turn the card over, and make the corresponding facial expression. The first student opens his or her eyes, observes the other students' expressions in the mirror, and guesses the emotion.

Meanwhile, the other small groups sitting in circles each receive a small bag which contains situation cards. Students in each group take turns picking cards from the bag and acting out the emotion. The rest of the group must guess the situation and the feeling it evoked. Some sample situation cards:

You are in pain as you ride the bus with a toothache.

You are frightened because you have just locked yourself in a dark room and can't get out.

You are happy because you are eating your favorite dessert: chocolate chip cookies and milk.

You are angry because you just missed catching a high ball and your team lost the game.

You are upset because your best friend, who is moving away, is saying good-bye.

Rotate groups so that each group has a chance to work in front of the mirror and get immediate feedback on their effectiveness.

Evaluation Criterion: Students' ability to convey emotion through mime.

Extension and Integration:

SPEAKING: Provide your students with many mime activities—a marvelous collection can be found in: Hennings, Dorothy. *Smiles, nods and pauses: Activities to enrich children's communication skills.* New York: Citation Press, 1974.

WRITING: Classrooms are places packed with emotion. From a list of emotions written on the board, have students choose one and identify the classroom incident during which the emotion occurred and its impact on others.

LISTENING: Read stories to the class and have students identify characters' feelings. Ask students to place themselves in characters' situations and decide whether their feelings would be similar or different.

FROM HAPPY TO SAD

Skill Area: Speaking
Pantomime (Creative Dramatics)

Background: The following activity asks children to experiment with a range of emotions, more specifically to shift from one emotion to another in a short period of time.

Objective: The student will pantomine a given situation to convey a range of appropriate emotions.

Materials: Cards with beach scenes (examples provided).

Activity: Give the class a good news/bad news line, such as, "The good news is that we're going to watch a film this morning (pause for reaction); the bad news is that there won't be any recess today."
Discuss the range of emotions and how students expressed them. Divide class into small groups and present each group with a beach scene which will evoke a shift in emotions. During their mimes, students are to concentrate on letting facial expressions and body gestures express emotions. No verbal communication is permitted.
Allow each group to work out their skit for 5–8 minutes. Possible beach scenes follow:

You and your friends are in the water, throwing a frisbee back and forth, laughing, and having a good time. Someone throws the frisbee out too far and the game ends.

Your friends are burying you in sand—covering your whole body except your head. Everyone is having a good time. Another friend comes along and invites everyone for a ride in his father's boat. Your friends leave you alone, buried in the sand.

You are in water up to your neck, watching your friends diving off a raft. Suddenly something touches your leg and you panic. You can't swim. You start sinking. You thrash your arms and legs around but you aren't moving. You start swallowing water. Your friends see you and pull you to shore.

You and your friends are waiting impatiently in line at the hot dog stand. Everyone is starving. You and your friends carefully carry your hot dog, french fries, and coke back to the blanket. Just as you are about to eat, a big wind sprays sand all over the food.

As each group performs, the audience is to pay close attention to the pantomimes and figure out the situation and its corresponding emotions.

Evaluation Criterion: Students' ability to use body movements/facial expressions to convey a range of emotions.

Extension and Integration:

LISTENING/SPEAKING: Popular TV shows—especially comedies—provide students with an excellent opportunity to watch actors express a range of emotions in a short period of time. Students can share their observations with the class, showing how emotions were conveyed.

LISTENING/SPEAKING: A number of Affective Education Programs such as *DUSO (Developing Understanding of Self and Others)* and *Focusing on Self-Concept* provide numerous activities to help children communicate and understand feelings.

Language: Prepare antonym cards:

Pass out one card to each student in a small group. Explain that one student will act out a word and the student in the audience who has the antonym to that word must stand up and mime the word. Students cannot show their cards to anyone else.

DRAMATIZING A
TARZAN STORY

Skill Area: Speaking
Dramatization (Creative
Dramatics)

Background: This stage of creative dramatics couples body movement with dialogue. Children act out the plots of familiar stories, usually under the direction of a narrator, using both movement and language to convey the storyline. The following Tarzan story was created to facilitate a wide range of movement and simple dialogue. A question and answer format is presented to "walk" the students through the process of dramatization.

Objective: Given a story stimulus, the students will dramatize assigned roles.

Materials: Copies of the Tarzan story (presented below) for each student.

Activity: Ask, "How many have watched Tarzan movies on TV? Where does Tarzan live? What's a jungle like?" Have students warm up by asking them to pretend the classroom is a jungle and getting them to move around the hot jungle. Ask what kind of animals live in the jungle. Have students move like lions, chimpanzees, birds, and other jungle animals. Ask students to pretend they are Tarzan, give the Tarzan call, and swing on a vine.

Read the following Tarzan story to the students and ask them to picture the various characters in their minds: How would they move? How would they feel? What would they be saying?

Deep in the jungle, Ted and his parents have stopped to take photographs of some rare birds. Just as Ted is taking his camera from his knapsack, he sees a chimpanzee. Without making any noise, he walks slowly toward the chimp, hoping to take a picture, but as he lifts his camera the chimp runs into the jungle.

Ted decides to follow him. The chimp moves quickly; Ted can hardly keep up. Running in a jungle is no easy feat! Finally the chimp stops to pick some berries, and Ted takes his picture. He is thrilled—no one else on the trip has been able to photograph a chimp. He excitedly calls to his father, "Dad, I did it! I got a picture of a chimp!" No one answers. Suddenly he realizes he is lost. He starts to run, then stops and looks around. He is frightened. He frantically calls for his parents. He runs through the brush until he is too tired to keep going. He's hot and hungry. He calls again, but no one hears him.

> Suddenly he hears a noise. He turns quickly to see a lion standing 5 feet away from him. He freezes, scared to death. The lion bares his teeth and roars at the boy. Just as the lion leaps toward the boy, Tarzan, swinging on a vine, gives his Tarzan call and lands right beside the boy. Tarzan tells the boy not to be afraid. The lion leaps at Tarzan. Tarzan throws the lion over his shoulder and the animal runs away.

To prepare the students for this dramatization, have them sit in a circle on the floor and discuss the characters and events and act out pieces of the story. You can begin the discussion by asking, for example:

1. How many have taken a photograph? Pretend you're taking one of me. What body motions would you use? What sound effects? (clicking)
2. What expression do you think the boy had when he saw the chimpanzee? Show me. (Encourage variety.)
3. How does a chimp move through the jungle? Show me.
4. What was the boy saying as he ran after the chimp?
5. Let your bodies show the fear the boy had when he realized he was lost. What did he say? Do? Now, say the lines while you show your fear.

Depending on student response, you may need to continue asking questions about the remainder of the story, helping them synchronize dialogue and movement.

Divide the class into groups of six to eight students. Pass out the Tarzan story and have the groups dramatize it. Encourage students not only to incorporate ideas expressed during the discussion, but also to create and act out new ideas.

Have students decide how roles will be assigned. Some groups may want to have a narrator who tells various parts of the story while the students act. Have the students practice their dramatization two or three times.

Emphasize that each time they rehearse the dramatization, it will change a little—the lines, the actions will be a little different—and that it's a sign of their growing confidence.

Have each group perform for the remainder of the class. Discuss performances.

Evaluation Criterion: Students' ability to dramatize a predetermined story with appropriate verbal and nonverbal expression.

Extension and Integration:

READING/SPEAKING: A wealth of material exists for story dramatizations: comic books, story books, basal readers, fairy tales, newspaper articles. Being able to act out what they read can spark a new interest in reading.

WRITING/SPEAKING: Now that Tarzan has saved the boy, what will happen? Each group can write a story ending and dramatize it for the class.

LISTENING/WRITING: Students can watch Tarzan reruns on TV and write scripts for use in dramatization.

PRETEND YOU'RE A TEACHER

Skill Area: Speaking Improvisation (Creative Dramatics)

Background: Improvisation is the ultimate form of self-expression in the creative dramatics process since it necessitates spontaneity of thought, imagination, and verbal and nonverbal expression. In the following activity, students are given school situations and asked to spontaneously create the dialogue and storyline.

Objective: Given a teacher scene, the students will improvise the dialogue and action.

Materials: Teacher cards (examples included).

Activity: Present the following situation to the class:

Ms. Hall, a third grade teacher, is standing outside the principal's office. She is very nervous because she has to tell the principal that she's taking the day off.

Prepare the students for this improvisation by first discussing the scene:

a. Why do you think Ms. Hall is so nervous about asking for the day off?
b. Why do you think she needs the day off? Is it a good reason?
c. How does a nervous person act? Talk? Find a partner, stand up and act very nervous; switch roles. Discuss variations.
d. What is the principal like? How does he talk? Walk? Act out the principal.
e. What will the principal say to her request?

Discuss how this creative dramatics activity differs from previous activities in that the actors will actually create the story as they go along—there is no script. Introduce the term *improvisation*.

Ask two volunteers to act out the above scene. Discuss the performance—their use of body language, ideas expressed, speech volume, and so forth.

Give everyone an opportunity to try an improvisation. Divide the class into small groups. Hand each group a teacher scene.

GYM TEACHER

Ms. McNally is leading the class in their exercises, however the students aren't working very hard. Ms. McNally has to find a way to get the class moving.

MUSIC TEACHER

Mr. DeMayo is teaching a new song to the class. A student starts making funny noises while he is singing. What happens?

CLASSROOM TEACHER

Ms. Buckley announces that it is time for lunch, but just before she finishes the sentence, three students dash to the door, knocking over the paint table. What happens?

PLAYGROUND DUTY

The class is playing baseball at recess. The students beg their teacher, Mr. Simonian to play with them. Mr. Simonian gets up to bat and the students cheer. He hits the ball so hard that it goes right through the school window. What happens?

Give students 5–10 minutes to work out their improvisation; encourage them to rehearse it a few times.

Have groups act out their scenes for the class and comment on what they liked about each others' performances.

Evaluation Criteria: Students' ability to create appropriate dialogue and action.

Extension and Integration:

WRITING: Students can use a magazine picture, a newspaper article, or a real-life experience as a stimulus for writing their own improvisation cards. Students can exchange cards and act out scenes.

SPEAKING: Present students with scenes which contain value conflicts and ask students to resolve the dilemmas through improvisation.

READING: Let students become actively involved in stories in their basal readers by having them read only the first part of a story. Students can then make predictions as to what will happen in the story and improvise accordingly. Students can then compare their version with the actual story.

SAY IT LIKE
YOU MEAN IT

Skill Area: Speaking
Oral Expression

Background: As students engage in a variety of speaking activities, the issue of oral expression will inevitably arise. The following activity helps children develop an awareness of the basic features of intonation and provides an opportunity for experimentation.

Objective: Given a sentence, the students will use various intonational features to convey the characters' emotions.

Materials: Situation cards (example provided).

Activity: Ask students to tell you what kind of mood you're in as you say the following sentence in an angry, controlled voice; say it slowly, pause frequently, and enunciate each word clearly:

> Put your books away, now!

As soon as students guess your mood, ask them to identify those features of your voice that lead them to their conclusion. Write students' responses on board and label them accordingly: volume, rate of speaking, pitch (high–low), stress, and pronunciation.

Explain that by varying volume, rate, and the like, the speaker can convey different meanings. Have the class experiment with alternatives, saying the above sentence in (a) a low quick whisper; (b) a loud laughing voice; (c) a normal voice.

Divide the class in four groups. Present each group with one of the following situations. Have each group discuss their situation and experiment with various voice qualities. Each group will then read their situation and perform the line:

> Let me out of here!

> Pretend that the janitor accidently locked you in the closet and leaves before you realized what has happened. It's dark. You hear a noise—something scurrying across the closet floor. You bang on the door and yell: Let me out of here!

> Now you have been in the closet for over an hour. Nobody has heard you calling. You can't stand the thought of spending the night in the closet with a mouse and you start to cry hysterically: Let me out of here!

> You've been in the closet now for 5 hours. You're so tired. You're hoarse from screaming but you must get someone's attention, so you call out again: Let me out of here!

> Suddenly you hear a noise—footsteps outside. You jump up joyously and shout for help: Oh, please let me out of here!

Evaluation Criterion: Use of appropriate intonational features.

Extension and Evaluation:

SPEAKING: Having focused on voice qualities, students can return to the scenes and dramatize them accordingly.

READING: Choral reading provides students with a perfect opportunity to experiment with oral expression. Students in groups can select characters from a basal story, practice reading their character's lines, and do a choral reading for the class.

READING: Once students have experimented with vocal features, they will be able to use this knowledge in their daily oral reading.

NEXT BEST THING
TO VENTRILOQUISM

Skill Area: Speaking
Oral Expression/Puppetry

Background: The success of a puppet show can, in part, be ensured if the children are encouraged to play with and develop the voice qualities of puppet characters. The following activity invites children to experiment with the voice qualities of popular TV characters, while their partners manipulate the puppet.

Objective: The students will prepare a short skit and employ voice qualities appropriate to the character.

Materials: Dracula puppet (sock puppet or paper bag puppet); Dracula skit (provided); materials to make puppets (socks, cloth, styrofoam balls, buttons, yarn, glue, needle, thread).

Activity: Prepare a Dracula puppet (sock puppet or paper bag puppet). Ask a student to practice the following skit with you. The student will be the interviewer who asks the puppet the questions. You will be the voice of Dracula. The student will synchronize the puppet's mouth movements with your words.

INTERVIEWER: (Looking at puppet) Well, tell us Count Dracula, where were you born?

DRACULA: (Slowly) In Transylvania, which is now Romania.

INTERVIEWER: When were you born?

DRACULA: In those days birth records weren't kept, but I believe I was born about 1430.

INTERVIEWER: (Sounding shocked) That's impossible! That would make you 550 years old. No one is 550 years old.

DRACULA: (Smiling) Well, there is a secret to my youth. Hrrrrrr (low, hoarse hiss).

INTERVIEWER: Yes, we know. You mesmerize a helpless victim and rob her of her blood. How do you do it?

> DRACULA: (Looking right at the interviewer) I hypnotize them with my eyes. Hrrrrrr (showing fangs). Watch! (Dracula hypnotizes the stunned interviewer and goes for the interviewer's neck!)

Before putting on the skit for the class, discuss ventriloquism. Explain that ventriloquism is an art that takes many years to master, but there is an enjoyable way to pretend that we are ventriloquists.

Perform the skit. Have the interviewer sit at a desk/table and rest the puppet on top. You will sit off to one side of the room (out of sight, if possible) and be the voice of Dracula.

Have students create their own skits and puppets with a friend. Students can think about characters on TV who have distinctive voice qualities, such as, Fonzi, Miss Piggy, Kermit, Yogi Bear, Mork, and so forth.

If possible, tape record portions of various shows to capture these voices and encourage children to listen to the recordings and approximate the voice qualities.

Encourage students to practice their skits on tape recorders so they can evaluate their effectiveness.

Evaluation Criterion: Use of appropriate voice qualities.

Extension and Integration:

READING/SPEAKING: The natural extension of the above activity is a full-blown puppet show complete with props and puppet stage. Most basal readers offer plays appropriate to students' reading levels.

LISTENING/SPEAKING: Members of the audience can become actively involved by listening attentively to the skits and asking the puppet some of their own questions.

SPEAKING: As a variation, students could take on the voice characteristics of various animals—lion (roaring), bird (chirping), snake (hissing)—and write and perform some creative skits interviewing animals.

READING: The story of Dracula continues to intrigue children and serves as highly motivational reading material. *Dracula* by Ian Thorne (Crestwood House, 1977) documents all the Dracula movies as well as the origins of this vampire and is written at a 4–5 grade reading level.

I HAVE A CONCERN

Skill Area: Speaking
Show and Tell

Background: Children are active consumers. Hours of television advertising are beamed at them by the toy companies, candy makers, and breakfast cereal producers. This simple show and tell activity will help raise their critical consciousness about the products they (or their parents) buy.

Objective: In an informal setting, children will describe the difference between how a television advertisement shows a toy and how a toy really operates.

Materials: Toys brought in by students.

Activity: As objects for show and tell, have children bring to class a toy or game that is popularly advertised on the television. Have each child recall with the group how the TV advertisement portrayed the game. (Children will likely be familiar with the ads.) Encourage children to also tell what the ad did not tell about the toy—what they expected the toy to do that it didn't. The children can also tell why they would or would not recommend this toy to friends.

Evaluation Criterion: The clarity and preciseness with which the child explains the differences between the television ad and the toy itself.

Extension and Integration:

LISTENING: Based on each speaker's presentation have members of the group ask further questions about the product.

READING: Call attention to the distinction between reality and fantasy, fact and fiction. This is an important critical reading skill. Discuss this difference as it relates to the show-and-tell object.

SPEAKING: Plan a follow-up creative dramatics activity, in which one pupil portrays a person in the complaint department of a toy factory or department store, while other children register complaints about their toys. Emphasize the amenities of speech in this activity.

WRITING: Have students compose simple business letters that might be written to the toy manufacturer or advertising agency, emphasizing points raised about the product during the show-and-tell activity.

READING: Bring in magazine ads for new toys. Have students raise questions about points that the ads do not address.

HAVE YOU SEEN
MY STITCHES?

Skill Area: Speaking
Show and Tell

Background: You slam your finger in a door and everyone comes running to see what happened. Instinctively, you show the bruise and explain the accident as those around you express concern and offer assistance. It's show and tell in its natural form. The following activity capitalizes on this topic of interest for both the speaker and the listeners.

Objective: The students will relate the sequential details of an accident and answer audience questions.

Materials: None.

Activity: Ask students to raise their hands if they have a cut, bruise, scar, or the like on their bodies. Comment on the frequency of accidents.

If possible, show and tell an injury of your own, detailing the accident and what was done. Remind students to listen carefully so that they can ask you questions later.

Encourage students to question you about the accident and praise their efforts: "Ted, that's a good question;" "Boy, I hadn't really thought about that, let me think."

Also compliment students on how well they listened; explain that their interest in your accident made you want to tell them all about it.

Ask, "How many would like to share their accidents with their classmates?" Stress the importance of taking a few minutes to think about their presentation which should include a description of the accident, who was there, and what was done.

Divide the class into small groups to maximize communication; first of all children are more at ease with small groups, and secondly children will turn off if they have to listen to a long string of show and tells.

Remind each group to listen carefully to its speaker so that questions can follow.

After each group has finished, pass out the following checklist to each member:

Did I think about my ideas before speaking?	Yes	No
Did I remember my ideas while I was talking?	Yes	No
Did I pronounce my words clearly?	Yes	No
Did I speak too fast?	Yes	No
too slow?	Yes	No
too loud?	Yes	No
too soft?	Yes	No
Next time, I'm going to _____		

Evaluation Criterion: The students' ability to describe a logical sequence of events.

Extension and Integration:

LISTENING: Tape recording each child's speech to the small group will provide him/her with important feedback on his or her oral language abilities. Using the tape-recording in conjunction with the self-evaluation checklist will allow the child to assess his or her effectiveness more accurately.

SPEAKING/READING: A logical follow-up to this activity would be a discussion/investigation around the issue of accident prevention. Students could explore safety tips for home and school and share findings.

WRITING: Students can send telegrams to speakers in their groups complimenting them on various aspects of their presentations.

FORTUNATELY/ UNFORTUNATELY

Skill Area: Speaking
Storytelling

Background: Most of us have heard "Good News/Bad News" jokes and many children are familiar with "Fortunately/Unfortunately" tales. (Fortunately, I took a plane ride. Unfortunately, the plane crashed. Fortunately, it crashed into a haystack. Unfortunately, . . .) This idea can easily be adapted for serial storytelling in the classroom.

Objective: Given a lead, students will tell part of a story in sequence.

Materials: None.

Activity: Ask students if they are familiar with the "Fortunately/Unfortunately" type of story. Have students who are familiar with this type of story share one briefly with the class. If students are unfamiliar, the one presented in the Background section can be expanded and shared.

Explain to the class that they are going to construct and tell a story in the same way, but that they are going to take turns in constructing the story one sentence at a time. A leader—the teacher or designated student—starts the first sentence. Some suggested "starters" are:

> Yesterday I met a man. Unfortunately, he had a gun. Fortunately, . . .
> A woman went hiking on a mountainside on a beautiful day. Unfortunately, the clouds suddenly covered the sun. Fortunately, . . .
> School vacation was coming and the family was going on a trip. Unfortunately, they couldn't decide where to go. Fortunately, . . .

After the leader provides this brief starter, he or she points to another student who then must follow this sentence in logical order. The second student points to another who continues and points to another until all students have had a chance to contribute to the tale.

As they are telling the story in turn, students should be aware of the rules:

- they must listen attentively to follow the story line as it is being constructed;
- each sentence must follow logically from the one preceding it;
- each pupil should be limited to one or two sentences, so that no one monopolizes the story;
- no one gets a second turn until everyone has had a chance to contribute.

Logical progression of the story line does not preclude imagination in the telling of the story. Logical progression means that each sentence must be related to the one immediately preceding it.

This type of serial storytelling is most often done in a whole-class setting. As a variation, the class can be divided into two groups, one handling the "fortunately" sentences and one the "unfortunately" sentences. The story starter can be written on the chalkboard and both teams might have a chance to brainstorm about all the pleasant/unpleasant things that could happen within the context that the story suggests.

Evaluation Criterion: Students' participation in completing the story.

Extension and Integration:

LISTENING: Inherent in this activity are opportunities for attentive and creative listening for all students involved.

WRITING: When everyone has had a chance to contribute to the serial story, each student can write his/her ending to the story. These results can be shared with other members of the class.

SPEAKING: As each student contributes his/her part to the story, each can act out the action he/she is relating.

STORYBOOK CHARACTERS COME TO A HALLOWEEN PARTY

Skill Area: Speaking
Oral Book Report

Background: Halloween and language arts—what a combination! Teachers' creative energies have children listening to spooky stories in a darkened room, writing stories about haunted houses with sound effects added, and sharing costume stories. The following activity adds a creative twist to the traditional book report by asking children to deliver the report, orally and in costume, from their favorite character's point of view.

Objective: The students in costume will deliver an oral book report from the perspective of their favorite character.

Materials: Halloween costumes—homemade.

Activity: At least one week before Halloween, role-play one of your favorite storybook characters for the class. For example, suppose you enjoy Max in Maurice Sendak's (1964) *Where the Wild Things Are*. You can costume yourself in a paper crown and cape. In your own words, tell the following story (in costume) to the class:

> "One day, I was running around the house and my mother called me a wild thing. I yelled back at her, and my mother didn't like that one bit, so she sent me to bed without supper. Soon my bedroom turned into a forest and an ocean and I sailed away to where the wild things live. The wild things roared at me and I told them to behave. The wild things were afraid of me and made me the king of the wild things. Soon, however, I felt lonely and decided to give up being king. I sailed back to my room and found my supper waiting for me."

At the end of your report, ask children to raise their hands if they know who you are. Discuss guesses. From a trick-or-treat bag, you can pull out *Where the Wild Things Are*.

Ask how many would like to dress up like their favorite character and tell the character's story. Suggest that this Halloween, instead of just buying costumes at the store, they can make costumes of their favorite storybook characters and come to the class's Halloween party.

To prepare the students for this activity, urge them to:

1. find a story-book character that they really like. Suggest that they go to the library and look over some of their favorite books before they make their final decision. Encourage them to talk to their family about the project. Stress the importance of keeping their character a secret so everyone except their family and the teacher will have to guess who they are. Have them discuss their character with you in private so that you can give costume suggestions and so forth.
2. keep the costumes simple—paper bag masks, old clothes will do just fine.
3. plan their character's story and rehearse it (on the tape recorder, if possible) a few times before Halloween.

Note: It may be advisable to develop an oral book report with the class. As an example, suggest that someone in the class selected a Wild Thing for their favorite character. Ask the class to tell the story now from the perspective of a wild thing. It might sound like this:

> "I live in the land of the wild things. The wild things roar terrible roars and gnash their teeth.
>
> One day Max sailed to our land. We tried to frighten him but he tamed us with his wand. We made Max, King of the Wild Things."

Emphasize the importance of story sequence.

On Halloween, let the storybook character party begin! Rather than overwhelm students with twenty oral stories in one hour, it is strongly recommended that the oral reports be spread out over the entire day; perhaps five at the beginning of each hour. This will help to assure attentive listening on the part of the audience. After each report, the audience can guess who the character is; the speaker can pull out his or her book from a trick-or-treat bag.

Evaluation Criterion: Students' ability to orally report on their favorite book from their favorite character's viewpoint.

Extension and Integration:

WRITING: This Halloween activity provides a great opportunity for students to practice their letter-writing skills. Students can write letters to the parents, explaining the big event, requesting help in story selection and costume making, and perhaps even inviting them to the party.

SPEAKING: Propose that students in small groups visit other classrooms and entertain students with their costumes and stories.

READING: One of the real benefits of this oral book sharing session will be the enticement of readers to new literature. It would be great to end this hectic day with a free reading period in which students can exchange favorite books.

FIRST AID TECHNIQUES

Skill Area: Speaking
Team Reporting

Background: The anxieties of oral reporting are reduced considerably when students are allowed to report as a team, each student taking responsibility for a small portion of the presentation. The following activity engages students in a mini-research project on the public service issue of first aid and results in a team presentation/demonstration of this important information.

Objective: The students will present the designated section of their team's report on first aid techniques.

Materials: First aid books.

Activity: If possible, recount an accident that recently occurred during school hours, such as:

> During lunch, a first grader started choking on a piece of food. Nobody knew what to do to help the child. Luckily the school nurse arrived right away. But what if she hadn't?

Ask students to relate other examples they have witnessed at school or at home. Suggest that everyone, the teacher included, would benefit from learning about first aid techniques.

Students working in pairs can select a first aid technique to research (nose bleeds, poisoning, choking, head injury, electric shock). Each team compiles its notes and organizes an oral presentation in which students:

a. identify the emergency;
b. explain signs/symptoms;
c. demonstrate the first aid technique.

As a practice session, students can tape record their report and evaluate their effectiveness:

1. Did I say my ideas clearly and accurately?   Yes   No
2. Did I pronounce my words carefully?   Yes   No
3. Did I speak too fast?   Yes   No
4. Did I speak too slowly?   Yes   No
5. Was my voice loud enough?   Yes   No

Because of the factual nature of information being presented, no more than three teams should present their first aid techniques per day. Students in the audience will have a much higher rate of recall if they are not overwhelmed with information. In addition, recall will be enhanced if teams ask members of the audience to practice specific techniques during class.

It is strongly recommended that the school nurse/doctor be present during the oral reports to ensure the information is medically valid.

Evaluation Criterion: Students' ability to present first aid information in a clear organized fashion.

Extension and Integration:

WRITING: Students can compile their information into a First Aid Handbook which can be used in times of emergency.

SPEAKING/WRITING: Discuss ways of preventing various accidents, such as, if you eat slowly, chew your food thoroughly, and refrain from putting small objects (buttons, coins, etc.) in your mouth, the risk of choking will be minimized. Students can create Prevention Posters and hang them around the school.

LISTENING: Learning how their bodies work will provide students with further insight into what actually happens during an emergency such as choking. Diagrams and films will enhance the explanation of how the body functions.

LIVING IN SPACE

Skill Area: Speaking
Persuasive Arguments

Background: Over the past decade, science fiction has sky-rocketed to popularity; adults and children alike can't seem to get enough of it. The following activity uses science fiction as its theme while focusing on the skill of oral persuasion.

Objective: Given six descriptions of space volunteers, the students will select four volunteers and give arguments as to why these four should participate in the space mission.

Materials: Six posters (described below).

Activity: Prepare six posters, each of which contains a picture of a person from a magazine and corresponding profile, such as:

```
┌─────────────────────────────────┐
│                                 │
│          ┌─────────┐            │
│          │ picture │            │
│          └─────────┘            │
│                                 │
│       NAME:   Lester            │
│        AGE:   44                │
│        JOB:   Judge             │
│                                 │
└─────────────────────────────────┘
```

Information for the five remaining posters is as follows:

NAME	AGE	JOB
Ronald	70	U.S. President
Maureen	38	Doctor
Pete	32	Baseball Star
Kathy	24	Teacher
Henry	12	Student

Prior to the presentation of the activity to the class, choose a student to practice the following role-playing situation with you:

Pretend you have a chance to go and live at the first U.S. Space Station. You want very much to go on this adventure, but you must convince you mother to let you go.

You can role-play the mother. Prompt the student to respond in the following fashion:

"I want to go."
"I hate school, I want to leave."
"I don't have any friends there."

Choose another student to participate in the same skit but prompt the second student to respond this way:

"It's the chance of a lifetime."
"It will be like a great adventure."
"I'll learn so much there, and I'll come back and study to be an astronaut."
"I'll be doing something important for this country."

Tell the class that they are going to observe two short skits about the same subject and decide which student's argument they like the best. Present the skits. Discuss student reactions. Explain that in order to persuade successfully, you must first appeal to the listener's needs/desire, and then convince the listener that your idea will make his or her desires happen.

Divide the class into small groups and propose the following task:

You are in charge of selecting a group of people who will be living on the first U.S. Space Station. Thousands of people have volunteered and all but six have been eliminated. Since the space station can only hold four occupants, it is your committee's job to select the four people.

Tape up the posters and read the profiles.

Explain that the members in each group will get a chance to argue persuasively for those candidates they feel should be finalists. Each group must come to a consensus and list their four choices.

Each committee should elect a discussion leader to keep the group on task.

Remind students that everyone is entitled to his/her opinion; no one should be criticized for voicing an opinion. The objective of the activity is for each member to come up with some good arguments for their candidates.

The group lists are collected and presented to class. Further opportunity for a class debate will arise if each group chooses different candidates. A class vote can finalize the list.

Discuss persuasiveness of arguments. Discuss how well students interacted; ask if discussion rules were violated and what effect it had on group performance.

Evaluation Criteria: The students' ability to persuade other members of the group by appealing to members' basic needs/desires and convincing them that their solutions will meet these needs/desires.

Extension and Integration:

SPEAKING: Rather than using posters designated in the above activity, six students could role-play the candidates and attempt to persuade the audience's decision.

READING: The activity should stimulate active interest in the U.S. space program. Students could research to find out if plans for space stations actually exist.

SPEAKING: Give students an opportunity to develop their powers of persuasion by presenting them with real-life situations: "You're tired of sharing your room with your brother/sister. Persuade your mother to think about giving you your own room."

SPEAK OUT!

Skill Area: Speaking
Persuasive Speech

Background: A persuasive speech challenges a student to identify an issue of importance, research the issue, and prepare a formal speech that will influence the thoughts and behaviors of the listeners.

Objective: The students will research a topic of interest and deliver persuasive speeches according to guidelines discussed in class.

Materials: Copies of a persuasive speech (example provided) for each student.

Activity: Deliver the speech outlined below to the class:

Shock Statement:	Does your mother smoke cigarettes? What about your father? Maybe you even have a friend who smokes cigarettes. Do you know how dangerous smoking is to a person's health? Do you know that smoking can even kill a person? That's right, smoking can kill you!
Problem:	In 1970, Congress passed a law that requires cigarette manufacturers to print this warning on the cigarette package label: "The Surgeon General has determined that cigarette smoking is dangerous to your health." Why? Because after years of research, doctors have found out that people who smoke cigarettes have a much greater chance of getting two terrible diseases: cancer and heart disease. These diseases can kill you. The problem is that millions of people continue to smoke everyday. They don't take the doctors' reports seriously. They are probably heading for real trouble.
Solution:	What can we do about this problem? Well, first of all, we can write to the American Lung Association and the American Cancer Society and get the facts. We can then bring these brochures home and ask people who smoke to read them and discuss the problem with us. We can give speeches on Parents' Night about the dangers of smoking and let our parents know we care about their health. We can pledge never to smoke ourselves!

Have students react to your speech. Find out how many were persuaded to join your no-smoking campaign and why the speech appealed to them.

Pass out copies of the above speech and explain the three steps in a persuasive speech:

1. The shock statement: Before you can persuade anyone to do anything, you must first capture their attention. Effective ways of opening a speech include asking questions, citing an illustration, using a quote, giving a shocking fact.
2. The problem: Identify the problem and explain how it affects the members of the audience. Use facts and figures to back up your speech.
3. The solution: Propose a solution(s) to the audience, suggesting a plan of action.

Encourage students to research an issue that is of importance to them and prepare an outline for their speech. Have students deliver speeches to the class (preferably one speaker a day) over a period of time.

Evaluation Criterion: The delivery of a persuasive speech that includes a shock statement, a problem, and a solution.

Extension and Integration:

WRITING: Students can write to various health organizations for free literature on harmful effects of smoking. Students can use the information in these brochures to create a Stop Smoking Bulletin Board which they can display on Parent-Teacher Night.

SPEAKING: Some of the students' speeches may be controversial in nature and their positions challenged by other students in the class. Formal debates can be organized to allow students to express their range of opinions.

LISTENING: A number of films on the harmful effects of smoking are available. In addition the school nurse/doctor can help students get a better understanding of these harmful effects by explaining exactly how tar and nicotine damage our bodies.

WRITING
ACTIVITIES

For years, reading and writing have shared the lion's share of instructional energy in the language arts. Children arrive at school fairly well in control of their ability to speak and listen. Schools, then, are faced with the task of helping them to become literate; that is, to develop in pupils the ability to read and write.

Of late, writing has become the object of intense criticism. "Why Johnny Can't Write" has become a rallying cry for educational critics and concerned citizens alike. This concern has caused educators to examine writing and how it is taught. Out of this examination has come new theories and techniques to improve pupils' writing skills. These theories and techniques are reflected in the activities that follow.

Throughout the activities, writing is seen as a *process*. Writing is not something that happens when the pupil picks up his/her pen (or pencil.) Rather, each piece of writing in which pupils engage ought to be preceded by a prewriting stage. This is a time for pupils to think about what they are going to write, what form it might take, and how best to present their ideas in writing. It's a time for pupils to reflect, to try out their ideas, to experiment with different techniques. The extent and quality of the writing will often be directly reflected by the thinking and discussion that go on in the prewriting stage.

Similarly, the writing process does not stop when the pupil writes the inevitable THE END at the conclusion of his or her story, essay, or other piece of written material. Rather, most formal writing experiences should be followed by a postwriting stage when compositions are reviewed, proofread, and corrected. Evidence indicates that through postwriting activities, pupils best develop and refine their ability to write.

All pupils should be given responsibility for proofreading the written products they produce. A proofreading guide similar to the following can be posted or duplicated for pupils:

- Are my ideas clear; in other words, have I said what I wanted to say?
- Are all my sentences complete? Have I used a variety of sentence types?
- Does each sentence begin with a capital letter and end with the right kind of punctuation mark? Are other punctuation marks where they belong?
- Are ideas grouped in paragraphs. Do I need more paragraphs? Are the paragraphs indented?
- Are all the words spelled correctly?
- Is my handwriting legible enough to be read by others?

Obviously, the standards and items in a list like this will differ according to the type of writing activity, along with the grade and ability level of the class.

In many ways, writing is the "pay-off" component of the language arts. That is, people are often judged—on a final exam, for example, or on a letter of application—on their ability to organize and present their thoughts in writing. The activities that follow have been prepared with an eye to making the "pay-off" worthwhile.

A WALK THROUGH THE WRITING PROCESS

Skill Area: Writing Stages

Background: We sometimes assume that giving students a writing topic—creative or otherwise—is enough to ensure a final product. It isn't. Writing is a complex, difficult process. We need to teach children how to write. We need to teach them that the actual writing of a story is only one step—the middle step—preceded by the prewriting step and succeeded by the editorial step. The following activity walks students through the three stages of the writing process and provides an opportunity for application.

Objective: The students will follow the three steps of the writing process as they draft a letter.

Materials: None.

Activity: Tell students that Parents' Night (or any other school event) is coming soon. Suggest that it might be a good idea to write a letter explaining the evening's events.

Explain that to write a good letter or a good story, it is important to follow three steps. Draw the following diagram of the three steps on the board (or even better, on chart for future reference):

Direct their attention to the first step, the *Think Step.* Explain the importance of thinking about what we want to write *before* putting our words on paper. To write a letter to their parents, they need to think about what will be included. Have students brainstorm information for the letter, such as the date, time, and place, as well as other things that may interest parents such as descriptions of the desks, papers on the walls, the classroom pet, and so forth. List their responses on the board. Since the ideas will probably be jumbled, have students reorganize them in a logical fashion.

Move on the diagram to the *Write Step.* Explain that once they have thought about what will be included in the letter, they are ready to put their ideas on paper. Have the students generate the body of the letter—have them concentrate on the ideas not on punctuation, spelling, and so forth, which comes later in the Edit Step. Either you or the students can write the first draft on the board or on an overhead projector. Remember that at this point, it is all right if students spell words incorrectly, overpunctuate, and the like.

When the first draft is complete, stress the importance of going back over the letter to see if any ideas have been omitted or to see if the ideas need to be reorganized. Deliberately omit an item and tell students that the item must be added. Have them figure out where to place this new information; using a caret (a mark that looks like an upside-down ''V'' and that indicates where to insert something), they can edit it into the letter. Explain that this is the last step in writing and it is called the *Edit Step.*

Explain that good writers edit their first draft for ideas, just as they have done. Next, it is important to edit for spelling; have them examine the letter for spelling errors and make necessary changes. Finally, have them edit for punctuation (and letter format).

Comment on all the changes made. Tell students they are now ready to copy over the draft in their best handwriting and bring the final product home.

As a follow-up, students can write a letter to you using their writing steps. The letter can explain the process a good writer uses to create stories, letters, and the like.

Evaluation Criteria: Students' knowledge of and ability to follow the three steps of the writing process while writing a letter.

Extension and Integration:

WRITING: Prior to any writing assignment, it is very beneficial to review the writing steps and even more important to allow students to spend sufficient time at each step. As an immediate follow-up to the first letter, students can be asked to write again to their parents, this time, asking how they enjoyed Parents' Night, what changes they would like to see, and so forth.

SPEAKING: As a way of enhancing the students' understanding of the prewriting stage (Think Step), propose the following writing assignment: Write about five things that you are proud of. Have students brainstorm all the various ways in which they could get ready for this report, for example: think about and list their achievements; talk to the family and friends; look through a photo album; consult their diary (if they keep one). Discuss the fact that writers get ready in different ways and that some writers need to think for a longer time than other writers.

WRITING: Return a writing sample (written before the introduction to the writing process) to each student and have them edit for ideas, spelling, and punctuation. The draft can be rewritten in final form.

EDIT-MAN

Skill Area: Writing
Editing

Background: To their dismay, teachers often find that children balk at the request to reexamine their stories and edit accordingly. Children dislike the task of editing because they seemingly equate it with failure or poor performance. Teachers need to emphasize that editing is integral part of the writing process, not a punishment. The following activity uses the format of the popular video game, Pac-Man, to actively engage children in the editing process.

Objective: The students will edit sentences for spelling, punctuation and grammar.

Materials: Edit-Man gameboard (guidelines provided); Velcro; an unedited story (example provided).

Procedure: Make copies of the story draft presented below for each student in the group; using the students' actual writing samples would also be very beneficial.

Edit -Man

Hi, My name are Edit-Man. I am Pac-Man bruther. I live in a maze like Pac-Man You probably know that pac-man spent his day eating Power Pills. vitamins. and Ghosts. I eating all day to. But I dont care for Power Pils. I eat sentences that have been correct edited. I wont never tuch a sentence that a punctuation mark miss- ing or a word mispelled !

Guidelines for preparing the Edit-Man gameboard, as shown in the illustration on the following page, are as follows:

1. Draw the black lines and the Ghost Cards section on a large piece of poster board.

2. To create the gameboard "spaces" (small black boxes) along which Edit-Man will move, stick small strips of Velcro on the gameboard.

3. Prepare two differently colored Edit-Men and attach a piece of Velcro to the back of each. Edit-Man will then stick to the "spaces."

4. Write each sentence from the above story on a separate strip of construction paper. Designate the number of points each sentence is worth (depending on the number of errors) in the corner of each strip. Laminate each strip and attach to the gameboard using small pieces of Velcro.

5. Construct a pack of Ghost Cards; examples are provided below. Place cards in the center of the board.

You need time to digest your sentences

MISS A TURN

You have just been clobbered by an Exclamation Point !

Go Back To Start

Pac-Man is visiting your maze today.

TAKE AN EXTRA TURN

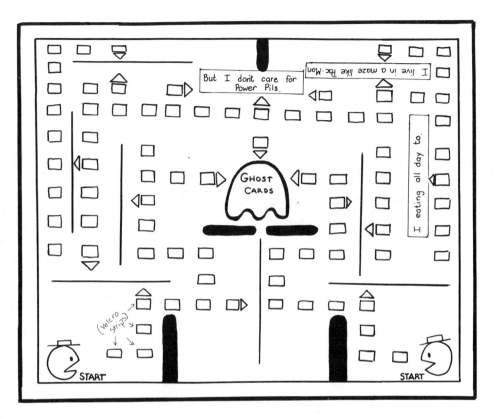

Ask how many students have played Pac-Man on a home computer or in the video arcades. Discuss Pac-Man's popularity.

Divide the group into two teams (2-3 players per team). Introduce the Edit-Man gameboard and read the Edit-Man story to the group. Pass out copies of the story to each team and explain that the story contains errors which must be edited. Review the editing process (see the previous activity, "A Walk Through the Writing Process" for details). Have the players on each team work together to edit the story, making the necessary changes on the copies.

Present the rules for playing Edit-Man:

1. Each team selects its Edit-Man and moves to the starting positions. A roll of the dice will determine which team begins.
2. The first team rolls the dice and moves that number of spaces; Edit-Man will adhere to that space. The players can move Edit-Man forward, backward, up or down.
3. The object of the game is to obtain as many sentence strips as possible and edit them correctly for the designated number of points. As soon as a team lands on a "space" with an arrow, the players remove the sentence strip and refer to their previously edited copy of the story. Using a grease pencil or marker, the players edit the sentence.

   a.   If correct, the team records the number of points earned and keeps the sentence.
   b.   If incorrect, the team wipes off their grease markings and the other team takes a turn. The first team can try that sentence again on its next turn or move off toward another sentence.
4. Each team may opt to take its changes and pick up a ghost card if the team lands on one of the three arrows surrounding the ghost cards. They must do what the card says.
5. The game ends when all the sentence strips have been removed. The team with the highest number of points wins.

When the game is completed, each of the edited sentence strips can be arranged sequentially and placed beside the original unedited version. The importance of editing can be reinforced through discussion.

   Evaluation Criterion: Students' ability to edit sentences for spelling, punctuation and grammar.

   Extension and Integration:

   WRITING: Another way to actively involve students in the editing process is to assign five students to play the role of "editors." As students in the class finish their story drafts, they can bring their papers to the "Editor Corner." Here the paper will be inspected by the five "editors." Two of the editors will evaluate the ideas of the story draft, asking the author questions about story sequence, plot, characterization and so on. The author can revise accordingly. The paper then passes to the "Grammar Editor" for comment, then to the "Punctuation Editor" and finally to the "Spelling Editor." Each editor, using a different colored marker, can underline errors. Papers are returned to author for correction and further rewriting.

   READING: The gameboard described in the above activity can of course be used to reinforce a variety of language arts skills. For example, sets of directions could replace the sentence strips. Students needing reinforcement in following directions could play the game according to the rules described in Edit-Man; instead of editing sentences though, students would read the directions and carry them out accordingly.

THE WRITING FOLDER

Skill Area: Writing
Creative Writing

   Background: The prewriting stage plays a critical role in the writing process. It is that time, before any words are put on paper, for students to allow their creative energies to flow in many directions, exploring all possible alternatives. The following prewriting activity uses pictures and questions to help children generate story ideas.

Objectives: Given a picture and corresponding questions, the students will write a story about the picture.

Materials: Oak tag folders, magazine pictures.

Activity: Prepare a number of writing folders that contain a variety of magazine pictures and corresponding questions. An example of a writing folder follows.

Before you start to write your story, think about these questions:

1. Who are the people in the picture?
2. Why are they at the pet shop?
3. How do you think the puppy feels?
4. How would you describe the puppy to your mother?
5. What will happen next?

These words may help you write your story: cage barking buy puppy pet shop

On the back of the folder, you can offer additional help:

If you are having a hard time getting your story started, try this: "Happy Birthday, Pat" smiled her father. "How does it feel to be eight years old today?" "Great" said Pat, "because I get my special gift today."

Introduce the writing folders to the group; explain that writing stories from pictures can be fun when they choose pictures that interest them or that look exciting. Explain also that most writers don't sit down and just start writing—writers need time to think about different ideas, about what they want to say.

Direct the children to the question section of the folder and explain its purpose. If time permits, ask the questions and encourage a range of responses.

Point to the list of words under the picture. Explain that the words are there for two reasons:

1. to give them more ideas about the pictures;
2. to provide the correct spelling of words that may be in their stories.

Explain that once they have read the word lists and have thought about the questions, they should be ready to write their stories.

For those students who are still having some difficulty getting started, direct them to the story-starter on the back of the folder.

Once their ideas have been expressed, direct students to go back and edit their stories.

Evaluation Criterion: Students' ability to generate ideas for a story from a picture stimulus.

Extension and Integration:

READING/LISTENING: Students may choose to read their stories to the class. Since the students have authored their stories no word recognition problems should occur; this will allow students to focus on their oral expression. Students should be encouraged to practice reading their stories a few times before reading to the group. The audience can be encouraged to actively listen to the story by giving them a general question such as "What do you think is the saddest part of the story?", or by giving them a specific question such as "What would you do if you were the father in this story?"

WRITING: Have the students make up their own Writing Folders. Working in teams/small groups, students can find a magazine picture which could translate into a good story. They should brainstorm and record a number of questions about the picture and select the best five questions from the group. Likewise a list of vocabulary words can be generated; dictionaries can be used to check spelling.

WRITING: Since the front cover of the folders are blank, children can be encouraged to think about illustrations for each writing folder. Titles can also be written on the front cover.

FRIENDSHIP AWARD

Skill Area: Writing
Creative Writing

Background: Writing about friendship is a very personal, meaningful experience. Ideas flow easily when the message matters. In the following activity, children are asked to recount special experiences shared with a friend.

Objective: The students will write friendship awards which recount experiences shared with a special friend.

Materials: A roll of newsprint, assorted art materials (buttons, yarn, paper, paints).

Activity: Say, "If you have a friend in this room, raise your hand." Comment on what a good feeling it is to have a friend and to have a class where people are friendly. Ask them to tell what a friend is, without telling their friends' names. Discuss responses. You may want to share your feelings about a friend or read one of the following books to the children to enhance the discussion:

BERGER, TERRY. *A friend can help*. Chicago: Raintree Editions, 1974.
NAYLOR, PHILLIS. *Getting along with your friends*. Nashville: Abingdon, 1980.
STEINER, CHARLOTTE. *A friend is Amie*. New York: Knopf, 1956.
ZOLOTOW, CHARLOTTE. *The new friend*. New York: Abelard-Schuman, 1968.

After the discussion, tell the class that they are going to have a chance to show their friends how much they like them.

Have friends, working in teams, create lifesize friend posters of each other:

1. Each student will ask a friend to lie down on a large piece of paper (or newsprint). The student will trace his or her friend's body outline. Students then exchange roles.
2. Each student will "dress up" (color/clothe) the friend's outline. Encourage creative use of assorted materials/objects: buttons glued on for eyes, yarn/painted macaroni for hair, etc.
3. Each student will design a Proud To Be Me button for his or her friend and paste it on the body poster.
4. For the finishing touch, the students will create a Friendship Award for his or her friend. Encourage students to first think about their friend—to think about experiences they have had together. Students can be directed to include the following in their Friendship Awards:
   a. a time when you were unhappy and your friend made you feel better;
   b. a time when you needed help and your friend was there;
   c. a time when your friend made you laugh so hard you couldn't stop.

Have students first write the drafts of their awards on scrap paper and their final drafts on "special" paper. Friendship Awards can be rolled up, tied with yarn, and attached to the body posters. Friends can then enjoy sharing their creations.

Evaluation Criterion: Students' ability to express thoughts about friendship.

Extension and Integration:

READING/LISTENING: The friend posters with awards attached can be hung around the room. Each day randomly choose four or five students to present their Friendship Awards to the class without mentioning his or her friend's name. Instruct the class to listen carefully so that at the end of the award, they can guess who the student's friend is.

LISTENING/WRITING: As students listen to their awards, they will learn much about their peers. Encourage students to listen to the awards for the purpose of finding a new friend. Students can write letters to their peers, expressing why they would like to start a friendship.

SPEAKING: Plan A New Friend's Day. New friends can get together and interview each other and perhaps put on a puppet show together about newfound friends.

SOUND STORIES

Skill Area: Writing
Creative Writing

Background: Another effective prewriting strategy is to ask students to listen to a series of related sounds and identify the sequence of events represented by those sounds. In the following activity, students are asked to turn a sound sequence into a story.

Objective: The students will identify a series of sounds and create stories related to those sounds.

Activity: Prepare a tape recording of common sounds heard around the house, school, or neighborhood. For example, a tape recording of a series of sounds associated with the classroom gerbil cage might include:

- placing a gerbil cage on the desk;
- cutting lettuce and carrots;
- opening a box of gerbil food;
- putting the food inside the cage;
- going to the water faucet and filling a water bottle.

Divide the class into small groups. Explain that they are going to listen to a series of sounds associated with the classroom gerbil. Play the tape, and after the tape has been shut off, have each group discuss the sounds. Replay the tape so they can confirm or reject their conclusions. Do not let the groups share their conclusions at this point.

Have the students in each group work together to write a story about the sounds (either literal accounts of what happened during the sound recording or imaginative accounts of what may have occurred during the recording). Encourage each group to edit the drafts for ideas, spelling, punctuation, and grammar. Have a member of each group write their final draft on large chart paper.

Have each group hang their story on the board. Compare results. Replay the tape and reveal the actual events. Some groups may not have accurately identified the sounds; let them know it really didn't matter because their stories were even more imaginative.

Evaluation Criteria: Students' abilities to identify the sounds and to compose a story based on what they hear.

Extension and Integration:

SPEAKING: Students can act out the actions associated with the sounds played on the recording.

READING: If the "sound stories" are written, students can read their stories aloud, with the sound effects playing in the background.

SPEAKING: Children can create their own sound sequences—live or on tape—as the basis for further "sound stories." Before engaging in this activity, they should meet in small groups to discuss what sequence of sounds they will make/record, who should have responsibility for what aspect of the activity, how they should proceed, and what they expect other children to do upon hearing the sounds that they make.

LET ME ENTERTAIN YOU

Skill Area: Writing
Creative Writing

Background: As preparation for the following writing activity, students actively peruse various sections of the Sunday newspaper to uncover wondrous possibilities for their imaginary trip. The students then describe each event in a brochure.

Objective: Given the Sunday newspaper, the students will write a brochure describing the events of an imaginary day.

Materials: Sunday newspaper; construction paper.

Activity: Ask students in advance to bring in a recent Sunday newspaper.

Ask students to share experiences in which their families planned a whole day of different activities.

Tell students that they are going to plan an imaginary day for a friend (in the classroom)—a day filled with exciting activities.

Ask students how they can find out what's happening in their town/city. Have them take out newspapers. Review the location and purpose of the Index by asking questions such as:

1. What's playing at the movies on Saturday afternoon?
2. Is there a baseball game on Saturday?
3. Suppose you want to take a harbor cruise, how much will it cost?

Explain that they are to pretend that they have $100 to spend for this special day. To enhance the complexity of the task, students can also plan meals, using food advertisements to calculate cost.

Students can draft out the schedule of events:

SATURDAY'S SCHEDULE		
TIME	**PLACE**	**COST**
9:00	Delicious McMuffin breakfast at McDonalds	$ 3.49
10:00	Relaxing boat cruise around the lake	$10.00 per person
11:00		

When the schedule is finished, students can calculate expenditures. If they have exceeded the $100 limit, adjustments in the schedule must be made, such as:

10:00	Rent mini bikes to cruise around the lake	$ 5.00 per person

When the scheduling is complete, encourage students to edit their drafts to make their schedules as inviting as possible. The final version can be written in booklet form, complete with illustrations. Friends can exchange their fantasy brochures and hope that one day it will happen!

10:00 am.

Time to rev-up your minibike for a spin around the lake.

11:00 am.

We set sail for a sunny cruise in the ocean.

Evaluation Criterion: Students' ability to write descriptions of exciting events, using the newspaper as a resource.

Extension and Integration:

WRITING: Have students write letters to parents requesting permission to bring in Sunday newspaper and explaining the writing project.

SPEAKING: Encourage students to talk with their friends, peruse the newspaper together, and so forth for mutually exciting activities.

READING/SPEAKING: Broaden the scope of the activity by bringing in brochures from various sites and encouraging students to read this literature in addition to the newspaper before making their schedules.

PERSONIFYING OBJECTS

Skill Area: Writing
Creative Writing

Background: Storywriting can be difficult for many children. Comments like, "I don't know what to write" are frequent. One easy story-starter that has been effective for a long time is to have students "get inside a common object" and to write a story from the object's point of view.

Objective: The students will write a story from the point of view of an inanimate object.

Materials: Common objects that can easily be found around the classroom or home.

Activity: Show the class an object with which they are very familiar—a postage stamp, a candy bar, the clock on the classroom wall. Ask students to pretend that they are that object and to guess what the object might be thinking at that very moment. Encourage students to suggest both realistic and imaginary responses. For example, a realistic response for the clock might be, "It's almost 2:30 and time to get ready to go home." A more imaginary response might be, "I wish these kids would get out of here so that I can get down off this wall and relax."

When students have had a chance to share response like these, have them write stories from an object's point of view.

Evaluation Criterion: Students' abilities to write a story from the object's point of view.

Extension and Integration:

SPEAKING: Have students tell rather than write such stories.

SPEAKING: As pupils tell their stories, or read the stories they have written, other pupils can act out scenes from the stories being told or read.

I WISH I WERE BECAUSE

Skill Area: Writing
Creative Writing

Background: Elementary school pupils (and pupils in the upper grades as well) often see history as a "dead" subject. Historical characters are to them dusty characters from the pages of books, not real people who actually lived. This activity is designed for the dual purpose of stimulating children's thinking and writing skills, while at the same time bringing historical characters alive.

Objective: The students will write real or imaginary accounts of historical figures.

Materials: Library reference resources.

Activity: Ask student to think about the following: "If you could climb into a time machine and go back to live in a long-ago era, what period of history would you choose? Who would you like to be in that time?"

Give pupils a few minutes to think about a possible response and perhaps let them share their ideas in small groups. At the top of the chalkboard, write the heading *I WISH I WERE.* Under this heading, write the names that pupils suggest, and as each pupil suggests a character, ask the pupil why he or she would like to be that character. Try to encourage pupils to think of real people; in other words, if a pupil responds, "I'd like to live in the 1950s and be Fonzie because he was cool," ask the student if he or she can think of anyone else who really lived in that era.

After pupils have dictated these basic thoughts, ask them to put their ideas into written sentences. Then have them add additional facts about the person. Pupils can either research facts to include in the selections they write, or they can write more imaginative accounts of their heroes, for example, "If I were George Washington, I would have . . ."

When pupils are studying a particular topic in social studies, they can be "assigned" to an era and choose the character within that era. For example, in studying the Pilgrim settlement, they could choose to be John Alden or Governor Bradford; with the explorers, they could choose to be Balboa, Magellan, Lewis and Clark, Sacajawea, or Cartier.

Evaluation Criterion: Pupils' completed real or imaginary accounts of their characters.

Extension and Integration:

WRITING: This activity applies directly to content areas of the curriculum. In addition to applications in social studies (suggested above), pupils can select from a list of scientists that the teacher provides.

READING   In locating information about each character, library skills are essential.

WRITING/DRAMATICS: A pair of students can team to write a dialogue or dramatize a hypothetical meeting between the two characters they choose; for example, an argument between Christopher Columbus and Amerigo Vespucci as to who discovered America. This may be especially interesting if the two characters are from different eras; for example, what might George Washington say to Joan of Arc?

MY AUTOBIOGRAPHY

Skill Area: Writing
Autobiography

Background: In writing an autobiography, a child is asked to capture on paper past experiences and incidents that are of personal importance. To prepare the child for this writing adventure, a variety of prewriting activities such as talking to family and friends, looking at old photographs, and creating a time-line of personal events are strongly recommended.

Objective: The students will write autobiographical booklets that reflect their personal time-lines.

Materials   Construction paper, paper plates.

Activity: Bring in a biography and an autobiography. Read the titles and authors, and ask if anyone knows the difference between the two terms. Discuss responses and explain the terms. Discuss why people write autobiographies.

Explain that students will have a chance to write their own autobiographies, but that first an introduction to the time-line concept is necessary as a way of helping them organize their information.

To illustrate a time-line, attach a long line about 2 inches wide and made of construction paper to the blackboard. Have a stack of paper plates ready.

Explain to the students that a time-line is a line that tells when important events happened. Order is important. Share important events of your own personal time-line or recreate one of a famous person. Record the date and the event (via words or pictures) on the paper plate. Spread the plates along the time-line according to the time span between events.

Have the children think about important events in their lives. Encourage them to share the project with their family and friends, talking about their early years, perhaps reminiscing with the family album.

Time-lines can be completed on a worksheet or on a model similar to the one presented on the blackboard. Moving from the time-line prewriting activity to the writing of the autobiography will be an easy task for most children.

Booklets can be created out of folded construction paper, one event (from the time-line) per page. Encourage students to illustrate their autobiographies. (Photographs, of course, would really enhance their final product.)

Evaluation Criteria: Students' ability to organize past events on personal time-lines and write autobiographical sketches from their time-lines.

Extension and Integration:

READING: During the reading time block, encourage students to exchange autobiographies. After reading, students can have a question and answer period about the events in the autobiographies they read.

READING: Display a number of published autobiographies in the classroom. Encourage children to read one or more of these autobiographies by periodically sharing background information about the authors.

LISTENING: Bring people from the community into the classroom and have them deliver an autobiographical sketch to the children which perhaps ties into a period being studied in social studies.

WHAT IT'S LIKE TO BE DISABLED

Skill Area: Writing
Diary Entry

Background: With the implementation of Public Law 94–142, disabled children have taken their place in the regular classroom, and teachers have begun to realize the critical importance of sensitizing students to the needs and feelings of their peers. The following activity is structured so as to allow students to experience various disabling conditions and write their reactions.

Objective: The students will choose one disabling experience and write a diary entry about this experience.

Materials: See each Center.

Activity: Set up the following centers in four areas of the classroom. Assign a student to each of the centers; it will be the job of these students to hand out materials, operate equipment, give directions, hold discussions. Divide the class into four groups. Allow 10–15 minutes for each center, then rotate groups.

CENTER A—I'M HAVING TROUBLE SEEING

MATERIALS: For each student at the center, have a Saran Wrap blindfold (take a 15–16 inch piece of plastic wrap, fold it over three or four times and staple ends together); a box of crayons; and a worksheet (provided).

ACTIVITY: The leader can ask each student to put on the blindfold and can hand each student a box of crayons and the following worksheet:

Name: _____		
Do you wear glasses?	Yes	No
Does anyone in your family wear glasses?	Yes	No
Have you ever seen a blind person?	Yes	No
How does being almost blind make you feel?		

Have the leader ask the students to write their names at the top of the paper with a blue crayon and to answer the questions with an orange crayon. When the students are done, they can remove the blindfolds.

Have students briefly share their feelings about their partial vision with their leader.

CENTER B—I'M HAVING TROUBLE HEARING

MATERIALS: A film; film projector; cotton balls.

ACTIVITY: Have students place cotton balls in their ears. The group leader can operate the film projector, showing about 5 minutes worth of film. Have students remove the cotton balls. The group leader, with questions about the film prepared in advance, can quiz the students about the film's content. (Be sure to have some questions that can't be answered by just *viewing* the film.) Have students briefly share their reactions to having a hearing impairment with their group leader.

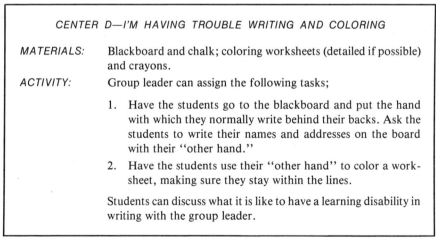

CENTER C—I'M HAVING TROUBLE MOVING

MATERIALS: Pieces of string; paper cups.

ACTIVITY: Have students line up chairs about 1 inch apart. Have the group leader give the following directions:

1. Sit on the floor and tie your legs together, not too tightly.
2. Now climb into your chair.
3. Now take this paper cup (handing one to each student) and find a way to get to the sink, fill your glass half way with water and get back to your chair.

Have students briefly share their frustrations of being physically handicapped.

CENTER D—I'M HAVING TROUBLE WRITING AND COLORING

MATERIALS: Blackboard and chalk; coloring worksheets (detailed if possible) and crayons.

ACTIVITY: Group leader can assign the following tasks;

1. Have the students go to the blackboard and put the hand with which they normally write behind their backs. Ask the students to write their names and addresses on the board with their "other hand."
2. Have the students use their "other hand" to color a worksheet, making sure they stay within the lines.

Students can discuss what it is like to have a learning disability in writing with the group leader.

After each group has had an opportunity to work at each center, have students return to their desks.

Ask students to choose one of the disabling conditions that made them think most about what it means to be handicapped. Ask them to pretend that they keep a diary and write about this experience in their diaries. In their diary entries, they can include:

a. their frustrations with the task;
b. ways they figured out to get around their disability;
c. how they felt about being disabled.

Students can volunteer to share their diary entries with the class.

Evaluation Criterion: Students' ability to write a reaction to one of their disabling experiences.

Extension and Integration:

SPEAKING: Have students talk about members of their family (or friends) who are disabled. Ask if they have ever been present when someone made fun of this person—how the disabled person felt; how they felt. Ask why people ridicule handicapped people and what can be done about it. Ask students if they should feel sorry for disabled people. Discuss the fact that disabled people don't want to be pitied but want to be understood and accepted.

LISTENING: *Feeling Free* is a series of Television tapes in which disabled children discuss their feelings about their disabilities. These video-tapes can be ordered from:

Workshop on Children's Awareness
22 Hilliard Street
Cambridge, MA 02138

READING: Through children's books, students may come to a better understanding of what it means to be disabled. The following books are suggested:

Hearing:

BROWN, MARION and CANE, RUTH.   *The silent storm.* Nashville: Abington, 1963.
PETERSON, JEANNE WHITEHOUSE.   *I have a sister, my sister is deaf.* New York: Harper & Row, Pub., 1977.
WOLF, BERNARD.   *Anna's silent world.* Philadelphia: Lippencott, 1977.

Vision:

CANTY, MARY.   *The green gate.* New york: D. McKay, 1965.
KEATS, EZRA JACK.   *Apartment No. 3.* New York: Macmillan, 1971.
WOLF, BERNARD.   *Connie's new eyes.* Philadelphia: Lippencott, 1976.

Physical handicaps:

DeANGELI, MARGUERITE.   *The door in the wall.* New York: Doubleday, 1972.
GREALISH, MARY JANE and GREALISH, CHARLES.   *Amy Maura.* New York: Human Policy Press, 1975.
LITTLE, JEAN.   *Mine for keeps.* Boston: Little, Brown, 1962.

Learning disabilities:

ALBERT, LOUISE. *But I'm ready to go.* New York: Bradbury Press, 1977.
HAYES, MARVELL. *Tuned in-tuned out.* San Rafael: Academic Therapy, 1974.
LASKER, JOSEPH. *He's my brother.* Chicago: Albert Whitman and Co., 1974.

FOR SALE

Skill Area: Writing
Descriptive Writing

Background: Children have a tendency in their writing to overuse words such as *nice, fun, happy*—words which add little to the image being created. The following activity encourages young writers to evaluate the effectiveness of the adjective, *nice,* and to brainstorm descriptive synonyms.

Objective: Given an unappealing for-sale sign, the students will rewrite the sign, making sure to include pertinent descriptive adjectives.

Materials: For-sale sign (example provided); construction paper.

Activity: Tape the following sign to the blackboard:

FOR SALE

Nice bikes for girls and boys. Each bike has a nice bag attached to the handlebars. These nice bikes give you a nice ride.

Buy a nice bike, NOW!

Ask students specific questions about the sign, for example, "What kind of bikes are on sale? Tell me about the bag that's attached to the handlebars. What kind of ride does the bike give?"

Discuss whether the sign gives a good description of the bikes on sale. Discuss the overuse of the adjective, *nice,* and its vagueness. Discuss the vital role of language in advertising.

Have students brainstorm adjectives that describe a bike. Write their response on the board.

Divide the class into small groups. Have each group draft a for-sale sign that would capture the attention of a prospective buyer. Stress the importance of pertinent descriptive adjectives as the groups edit their drafts. When each draft is in its final stage, students can design their for-sale signs, complete with illustrations.

The signs can be displayed and evaluated for their descriptiveness.

Evaluation Criterion: Students' use of pertinent descriptive objectives.

Extension and Integration:

READING: Have students locate bicycle ads in magazines and examine the methods professional advertisers utilize to create ads. Comparisons can then be made between their ads and the advertisers' ads.

READING/WRITING: Discuss how descriptive adjectives enhance any piece of writing. Have them read a passage from their basal readers and count the number of times a descriptive phrase is used. Challenge the students to rewrite the passage, making it even more descriptive.

WRITING CAPTIONS

Skill Area: Writing
Descriptive Writing

Background: Children see pictures all around them—in newspapers and magazines, in books and on posters, in advertisements and on cereal boxes. These pictures often have captions and the captions describe or explain what is happening in the picture. Writing captions for pictures requires specific skills that include descriptive and concise writing.

Objective: The student will write captions for magazine pictures.

Materials: Pictures clipped from newspaper or magazines; one large poster.

Activity: Tape a large poster to the chalkboard or call pupils' attention to a poster that may be on display in the classroom. Have pupils describe what they see in the picture on the poster. Stress the importance of selecting vibrant, specific words to describe the scene or action depicted. The words will obviously differ in describing the power and grace of an athlete or a dancer, the peace and tranquility of a nature scene, or the incongruity and fun of a more humorous poster.

Invite pupils to dictate what they would consider an appropriate caption

for the poster. If the poster already contains a caption, have pupils suggest alternatives. Encourage pupils to explore different styles of writing in the captions they suggest. For example, for a poster depicting a skier skiing down the side of a mountain, the captions might be:

Narrative: Typifying the increasing popularity of this winter sport, a lone skier moves gracefully down the side of a mountain.

Descriptive: White powder spewing from the sleek surface of his skis, the speedy skier plummets down the snowy slope of the mountain.

Humorous: Oh, no! I just missed that last tree and I truly hope that there are no more trees ahead.

A variety of different tones and different voices should be encouraged. Distribute pictures clipped from magazines or newspapers and have pupils write captions for these pictures. As part of the prewriting discussion, pupils should be made aware that the caption must be written in precise, concise terms. Placing a limit on the number of words to be used may be appropriate.

After pupils have had a chance to share their pictures and captions with the class, a bulletin board of the pupils' writing can be made.

Evaluation Criteria: Pupils' completed captions for their pictures.

Extension and Integration:

ART: Pupils can write captions for drawings that they create during art class. Similarily, pupils can select short prose passages or poems that describe an object or a scene and, using what they have chosen as a caption, draw a picture depicting the scene described in words.

VOCABULARY: As pupils are examining their pictures in the prewriting stage, specific attention should be devoted to appropriate word choice. Pupils can list several verbs that can be used to describe the action in the picture, and several adjectives to describe the people and places depicted. Careful word choice should then be exercised in writing the caption.

VOCABULARY: Pupils can be assigned to find pictures in newspapers and magazines that illustrate abstract terms. Word selection can, for example, focus on emotions, and pupils can locate pictures to illustrate words such as *joy, fear, hatred, love,* and so forth.

WRITING HAIKU

Skill Area: Writing
Poetry

Background: Haiku poetry—the three-line Japanese verse form that has five, seven, and five syllables respectively per line—has long been popular in American classrooms. Children will come to a greater understanding and appreciation of haiku, however, if they understand that this syllabic arrangement is not arbitrary. Haiku is a poetic form with purpose and with a centuries-old tradition.

Objective: Children will write haiku poems expressing their appreciation of nature.

Materials: None.

Activity: First, since nature is (or should be) the subject of haiku, this activity should be planned at a time when pupils' attention is focused on nature. Suggested times might include the first crisp day of fall, the first snowfall of the season, a violent thunderstorm, or a follow-up to a story on natural wonders.

As part of prewriting discussion, explain that haiku is a literary form that can be traced back to the thirteenth century and that has its roots even further back in the eighth century. Haiku has deep cultural and religious ties with Zen philosophy, which believes that humans and nature are closely related. Haiku is an expression of this kinship between nature and humanity.

Explain the form of haiku; that is, that it contains three lines, the first line has five syllables, the second line has seven syllables, and the third line contains five syllables. Write one or two models on the chalkboard, for example:

Puffy cotton clouds
Billowing across the sky
Rushing to a storm.

Stately trees stand tall
Guard the entrance to the path
Silent sentinels.

While haiku demands a certain structured form, pupils should understand that each verse should be a momentary expression of appreciation for nature, a "breath-long expression of delight." The seventeen-syllable length of each poem is the typical length of a spoken expression. Pupils should also understand that haiku is a subtle form of poetry that is intended to suggest rather than to state. Finally, pupils should understand that haiku doesn't have to rhyme at the end of the line.

With introductory models, pupils should have enough time to produce and share original haiku poems. The results, appropriately illustrated, make an effective bulletin board display.

Evaluation Criteria: Pupils' completed haiku.

Extension and Integration:

READING: Pupils can read published or peer-produced collections of haiku.

LANGUAGE: A list of words that might be used to describe nature might be written on the chalkboard to be used in writing haiku.

SPEAKING: As a stimulus for writing haiku, selected pupils can describe for the class natural scenes with which they are familiar. These can be used to stimulate other pupils to write haiku. In these descriptions, the emphasis needs to be placed on vivid detail (for the speaker) and on listening skills (for the audience).

MAKING SENTENCES GROW

Skill Area: Writing
Sentence Combining

Background: Research has proven sentence combining to be an effective way to help pupils of all levels improve their writing ability. Based on the theory of transformational grammar, it involves putting basic kernel sentences together in a variety of ways.

Objective: Pupils will combine five basic sentences into a single sentence in at least two different ways.

Materials: A list of basic sentences.

Activity: Write two simple, basic sentences on the board or on an overhead transparency; for example:

I have a dog.
His name is Fleas.

Ask the class to think of ways to combine these two sentences into one longer, more mature sentence. As pupils suggest ways of combining these sentences, copy the sentences they suggest:

I have a dog and his name is Fleas.
I have a dog whose name is Fleas.
I have a dog named Fleas.
My dog is named Fleas.

Call pupils' attention to the different ways in which these sentences were combined. If pupils have been introduced to grammar, terms like *prepositional phrase* and *dependent clause* can be reinforced in the discussion. Then add two more sentences to the list and ask pupils to combine the four sentences into a single sentence, for example:

I have a dog.   He is brown.
His name is Fleas.   I play with him after school.

Transcribe and discuss the various combinations that children suggest, for example:

I have a brown dog whose name is Fleas and I play with him after school.
After school, I play with my brown dog Fleas.

Once again, call pupils' attention to how these sentences are combined. Follow the same procedure with additional basic sentences added to the list, or begin a new list on a new topic.

Lists of basic sentences for sentence-combining practice can be generated from several sources; for example,

From the view from the classroom window: We look out the window. We see trees. We see a hill. The hill is covered with snow. A dog is running in the snow.

From a shared class experience: We walked around the school. We met the principal. We saw the kindergarten class. They were in their classroom.

In response to a book or a story that the class may have read: We just read *Grandma Didn't Wave Back*. It was a sad story. It was about a girl and her grandmother. They lived together.

When sentences are combined in a variety of ways, the class should examine the newly generated sentences to decide which forms are most efficient and effective.

For the best effect on pupils' writing, sentence combining practice should be provided on a regular basis during the week.

Evaluation Criterion: Pupils' ability to produce well-written sentences in a mature style.

Extension and Integration:

READING: Research indicates that the practice of sentence combining itself improves pupils' reading comprehension. Having explored the relationship of syntactic units in writing sentences, pupils are better able to understand such relationships in reading sentences.

READING: Pupils can gain practice in oral reading by reading the sentences they write to the class.

LISTENING: As one pupil reads his/her sentence to the group, other pupils should be directed to listen attentively to be able to repeat the sentence verbatim.

DISCUSSION: Standards of classroom discussion should be adhered to as pupils discuss which sentences are most effective and efficient.

A SATURDAY MORNING SEQUENCE

Skill Area: Writing
Sequential Order

Background: This is the first of a two-part series on sequential order. Sequencing events is a necessary ingredient in good story writing. To grasp this concept, children need opportunities to put events in order and offer a rationale for doing so. After sequencing the events in "Sam's Saturday Morning," students are asked to write their typical Saturday morning schedule.

Objective: The students will write four Saturday morning events in sequential order.

Materials: Four sets of sequenced pictures (example provided).

Activity: Prepare four sets of three sequenced pictures as shown in the illustration. Suggestion: For the bedroom scene take three pieces of yellow construction paper and reproduce the pictures and sentences; use three pieces of pink paper for the bathroom scenes and so on.

Draw a house on the blackboard, with each "room" large enough to hold three pieces of construction paper.

(As an alternative to this preparation, the illustration may be copied and passed out to students. Students can then number each picture to indicate the appropriate sequence for each "room.")

Ask students to describe what they do on Saturday morning. As students respond, try to establish the concept of sequence by asking: "Is that the first thing you do on Saturday morning or the last? What do you do after that?"

Tell the students that they are going to have a chance to compare their Saturday morning with Sam's. Direct the student to Sam's house and present the first set of pictures; have students figure out that the order is incorrect. Students can volunteer to sequence the scenes.

Move on to the next room and repeat the procedure, making sure they are grasping the concept of sequencing. Use the sequence words *first, second, then, finally, next* as frequently as possible.

Ask students to explain how their Saturday mornings are different from Sam's. Give students an opportunity to illustrate their Saturday morning se-

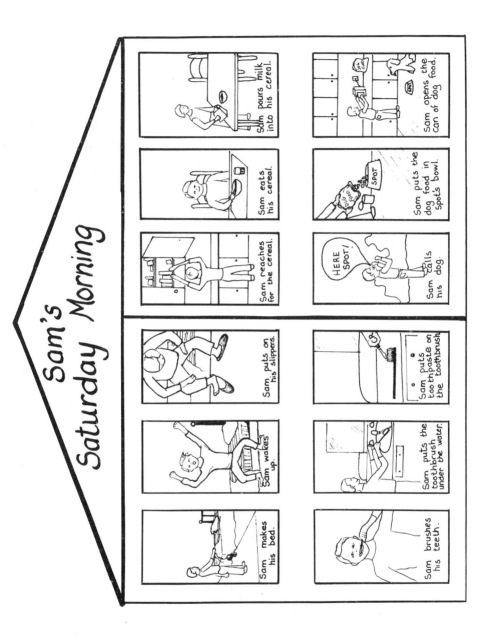

quence. Pass out a worksheet, similar to Sam's house with the four blank spaces representing rooms. Have students think about the order of events of a normal Saturday morning at their house. In each "room" the student will write about one event in the sequence and illustrate it.

Evaluation Criterion: Students' ability to sequence four events in their typical Saturday morning.

Extension and Integration:

SPEAKING: Let students share their Saturday mornings with each other. In addition, a Saturday morning survey can be taken by the students; for example, on Saturday morning: How many get up and go right to the T.V.? How many get their own breakfast? How many get up and go outside without eating breakfast?

READING: Comic strips provide teachers with readymade sequencing materials. Comic strips, appropriate to the students' reading level, can be cut up and scrambled. Students will enjoy placing the frames back in their proper sequence.

WRITING: Sequencing is an important part of giving directions. Students can practice sequential writing by creating directions for a wide variety of "How To" tasks:

a.   How to brush your teeth.
b.   How to plant a seed.
c.   How to make a tie-dye shirt.
d.   How to get from the school to the library.

AND THEN THE UNEXPECTED HAPPENED

Skill Area: Writing
Sequential Order

Background: Once students have grasped the concept of sequential order, instruction needs to be carried one step further. Students need to understand that good story writing is more than a string of sequential events—that something unexpected must happen during one of the events that completely alters the story ending.

Objective: Given events from Sam's Saturday morning, the students will select one event and build a sequential story with an unexpected turn of events.

Materials: A review worksheet on sequencing (example provided); an event in a story with an unexpected twist (example provided).

Activity: To review the concept of sequencing, have students complete the following worksheet.

DIRECTIONS: Sam has six important things to do next Saturday. Unless Sam plans to do things in a certain order, he's not going to be able to fit everything in. Help Sam out. Place a number in each blank space to show the order Sam must follow.

_____ play a ballgame from 10:00—11:00.

_____ get his hair cut at the barber shop which is open from 9:00—12:00.

_____ deliver his morning papers (on his bike).

_____ watch a special T.V. show at 12:00.

_____ take a tennis lesson from 9:00—10:00.

_____ fix the flat tire on his bike.

Discuss students' sequences. Challenge their responses: "Why can't Sam do his paper route after the T.V. show is over?" "Shouldn't Sam get his haircut before he plays baseball?"

Now students are ready to write a story about Sam's morning. Have students as a group dictate the story, while you write it on the board. Most likely, their story will be little more than a listing of the six events. At this point it is important to stress that a good story needs not only a sequence of events but also a story plot in which something unexpected happens.

To illustrate, take one of Sam's events; for example, getting a haircut at the barber shop. Have students identify the normal sequence of events at a barber shop and brainstorm a possible turn of events. For example:

Sam is waiting at the barbershop, watching the barber shave the head of the boy in front of him. Sam panics. He doesn't want the barber to shave his head, so he leaves. What is he going to do now? He promised his mother he'd get a haircut. Then Sam comes up with an idea: why not have his sister, age 12, cut his hair!!!

Divide the class into five groups, each group selecting one of the five remaining events from the worksheet. Instruct each group to write a story about the event which contains a story plot with a clear sequence of events.

Evaluation Criteria: Students' ability to write a sequential story that contains an unexpected turn of events.

Extension and Integration:

READING/LISTENING: Have a student from each group read his story to the class. Instruct the audience to listen carefully and count the number of events in the story. The class can then try and recreate the sequence.

LISTENING: Read a story and have students illustrate the sequence of major events; in addition have students identify the events in which something unexpected happens. For younger children, it is helpful to read/tell a story in conjunction with four or five pictures. After the story, mix up the pictures and ask the children to sequence them.

READING: Students can follow a set of written directions on how to make/cook something. The directions should be such that if the students don't follow the prescribed sequence, the activity will flop.

SUPERHEROES

Skill Area: Writing
Story Plots

Background: The Villain plots a diabolical crime, the Superhero battles the Villain but is temporarily thwarted by the Villain's tricks and traps, and in the end justice prevails. Such is the predictable plot of the Superhero stories—a predictability that easily lends itself to analysis by children. The following activity introduces children to plot predictability and encourages them to use the plot pattern as a model for their own Superhero stories.

Objective: The students will write Superhero stories, paying particular attention to plot development.

Materials: Worksheet of Superhero characters (example provided).

Activity: Play "Guess who":

"Who is faster than a speeding bullet?" (Superman)
"Who pilots in an invisible plane?" (Wonder Woman)
"Who weaves a net to catch a criminal?" (Spiderman)

Ask how many watch the Superheroes on T.V. Have children identify their favorite Superheroes. List names on the board.

Ask students why they like watching the Superheros. As students respond, emphasize two important features of a good story: characterization and story plot. Explain to students that they'll have a chance to write Superhero stories as soon as they gather more information about the characters and story plot.

To collect background information on the Superheroes, pass out the following worksheet and have students examine and comment on the Superman data:

121

SUPERHERO	SUPER POWERS	WEAKNESS	MAJOR OPPONENT/ VILLAIN
Superman	Super strength Super hearing X-ray vision Flies, leaps tall buildings Spans time zones	Kryptonite	Luther
Wonderwoman			
Batman			
Spiderman			

Students, in small groups, can generate information for the remaining Superheroes (students' preferences for specific Superheroes can be substituted on above worksheet). Let students know that they may not be able to fill in all of the boxes and not to worry. Upon completion, groups can discuss their charts.

Perhaps the easiest way to explain story plot or story action is to draw an analogy between a plot and a roller coaster. Ask a student to retell a Superhero story he or she has watched on T.V. as you diagram it in the following fashion:

Batman & Robin
battle the Penguin

Penguin plans diabolical crime

Batman & Robin free themselves and thwart the Penguin

Penguin traps Batman & Robin

Average day in Gotham City

Penguin lands in jail

Explain that a story plot is like a roller coaster—it starts out slowly, builds up speed, explodes with excitement and then winds down. Discuss how all Superhero stories follow the same plot:

Average day	Villain plots his/her crime	Superhero battles crime	Superhero trapped	Justice wins out— Superhero freed and stops crime

Instruct students to think up a diabolical crime (brainstorming crimes may be necessary for some students) and use their Superhero chart to weave together a good storyline. Some students may find it helpful to diagram (on the roller coaster) their story plot before putting the story on paper. Have students proofread their drafts and edit for ideas, language, and the mechanics.

Evaluation Criterion: Students' ability to develop plots for their Superhero stories.

Extension and Integration:

SPEAKING: Creative dramatics is a must here. Students can create Superhero costumes and possibly some special effects for their dramatizations.

LISTENING/WRITING: Students can watch Superheroes shows on T.V. to discover new superheroes and add them to their charts. In addition, students can design crime cards, which summarize the various villainous schemes found on the T.V. shows.

READING: Comic books provide a great source of entertainment. Students can read Superhero comic books and diagram the plots.

GUIDE TO THE T.V. GUIDE

Skill Area: Writing
Plot Summaries

Background: To create the *Guide to the T.V. Guide* students are asked to analyze the predictable plots of popular T.V. shows and write concise summaries. Since students will be working with partners, they will have a marvelous opportunity to work through each stage of the writing process, examining each others' ideas and drafts, and reaching agreement on the final product.

Objective: The students will identify major characters of certain T.V. shows, summarize the shows' general plots, and write their reaction to these shows.

Materials: Copies of *T.V. Guide;* an entry page (example provided).

Activity: Pass out an index card to each student. Ask students to write down the names of two T.V. shows that they haven't watched but would like to at some time in the future. Collect the cards (this could be done just before recess so that during the time break a small group of students could be asked to relinquish their recess and compile the results).

Present the results to the class—listing ten to fifteen T.V. shows on the board that have been viewed by some portion of the students.

Discuss the idea that people often get into the habit of watching certain shows to the exclusion of others.

Propose the idea of a *Guide to the T.V. Guide* as a way of broadening the group's viewing habits. Pass out the following entry page and explain:

Suppose you have never watched the *Incredible Hulk* but would like to know what it is about. You would go to the *Guide for the T.V. Guide* and look under "I" for *Incredible Hulk*. On that page you would find the following information:

T.V. Show: Incredible Hulk   *Time: 8:00—9:00 P.M.*
Day: Friday   *Channel: 7*
MAJOR CHARACTERS

> *David Banner*—a scientist who experimented with human strength and accidentally received a dose of gamma rays which changes his body into the Hulk when he gets angry. David runs from town to town so no one will discover his Hulk identity.
>
> *The Hulk*—A huge green monster-man who is really David Banner. The Hulk is wanted for murdering David Banner.
>
> *Mr. McGee*—A reporter who follows the Hulk, wanting to capture him and turn him over to the authorities.

GENERAL PLOT

David Banner arrives in a new town and finds a job.

He makes friends quickly and is ready to help his new friends when trouble comes along. When David fights with his friends' enemies, he usually hurts himself. This makes him very angry. In his angry state, he turns into the Hulk and scares away the enemies.

Meanwhile Mr. McGee hears about the Hulk's whereabouts and arrives in the town. When David realizes that McGee is on his trail again, he packs up and heads for a new town.

RECOMMENDATION

Excellent show. David Banner, played by Bill Bixby, is a very good actor. The Hulk really is incredible. The show has a lot of action.

Discuss components of the preceding entry page:

1. Explain the difference between major and minor characters. Have students comment on whether any characters have been omitted.
2. Review the concept of story plot (see previous activity, "Superheroes," p. 121). Be sure children understand that while specific incidents and (minor) characters change, the storyline of most T.V. shows remains the same. Students can read the general plot for the *Incredible Hulk* and determine if all major parts have been included. It would be beneficial to select another T.V. show and have the whole class summarize the general plot, to ensure that everyone gets the idea.
3. The recommendation section allows students to critique the shows. A list of questions may be a helpful guide; for example:
   a. What do you like/dislike about the actors?
   b. Is there a lot of action?
   c. If it's a comedy, are the lines funny?

When students understand the format, group them into teams by pointing to a show listed on the board and asking those students *who have* watched that show at least twice to raise their hands. Select two or three students for each team.

Have copies of *T.V. Guide* available for reference. Compile alphabetically all the students' entries into one booklet, titled *A Guide to the T.V. Guide.*

Evaluation Criteria: Students' ability to complete entry pages with appropriate information about T.V. characters, plot summaries, personal reactions.

Extension and Integration:

READING/SPEAKING: Propose a New Show Week: everyone, including the teacher is to consult the *Guide to the T.V. Guide,* select a show they have never watched for viewing. On the following day, students (and teacher) can share their reactions and comment on the accuracy of the entry they read in the *Guide.*

SPEAKING/WRITING: Discuss various categories of T.V. shows, that is, comedy, drama, documentary. Make a poster which is divided into columns, each column having as a heading, one of the discussed categories. Have students consult T.V. guides and categorize popular shows accordingly.

READING/SPEAKING: Have students talk about shows they watched when they were "younger," or shows that younger brothers and sisters presently watch. Have students compile a list of recommended shows for younger children. Students can then visit the younger grades and talk about shows on their lists.

ESP

Skill Area: Writing
Main Ideas

Background: In writing reports, children frequently get lost in the myriad of details, with no effective strategy for organizing their information. The following activity introduces children to the concept of main idea, first through pictures, then paragraphs.

Objective: Given three paragraphs, the students will write a main idea appropriate to each paragraph.

Materials: Magazine pictures; picture titles on strips of paper; paragraphs (examples provided).

Activity: Prepare three sets of magazine pictures; each set should contain three pictures.

1. The first set of pictures should depict three different settings, such as, a beach scene, a school scene, a store scene. Write a title for each picture on separate strips of paper.
2. The second set should contain two pictures, similar in nature, such as, two street scenes and a restaurant scene. Write titles on separate strips of paper.
3. All three pictures of the last set should depict the same scene, such as three pictures of baseball games, each with a somewhat different focus. Write titles on separate strips of paper.

Tape the first set of pictures on one side of the board and the three titles off to the side:

Pictures   Titles

Have the students examine pictures and match corresponding titles.

Repeat procedure with the second set of pictures. Ask how this set was a little more difficult. Since there were two street scenes (or whatever), how did they know which title went with which picture? Explain that titles are the main ideas of the pictures; titles tell what the picture is about but they don't include any specific details.

Explain that the last set of pictures is even harder, but as long as they figure out the main idea of each picture, they'll be able to make the match.

Tape up a new picture and have the students provide the title. Some students may get too specific; remind them that the main idea tells what the picture is about.

Explain that paragraphs are like pictures; they both contain main ideas and details. Write the following information on the board:

Dr. Rhine coined the term ESP.	Many people think ESP doesn't exist.	There are three types of ESP.

The first type is called *telepathy.* It means that you can read the mind of another person. *Clairvoyance* is another form of ESP. If you are clairvoyant you can see things that are taking place somewhere else. The third type of ESP is known as *precognition,* which means seeing the future in your mind before it happens.

Have students read the details and select the appropriate main idea. Ask why the other two sentences cannot be the main idea of this paragraph. Emphasize how details support the main idea.

Pass out a worksheet with the following paragraphs. Explain that the main ideas are missing. Having the students fill in a main idea for each passage. Discuss results.

Main idea:

Have your friend look at the top card, write down the color (red or black), Number two sheets of lined paper from 1 to 52. Give one sheet to your friend.

Have your friend look at the top card, write down the color (red or black), and tell you through mental telepathy what the color of the card is.

You write down the color that comes to your mind. Go through the entire deck. If you guess thirty or more correctly, you may have ESP.

Main idea:

A story is told that President Abraham Lincoln had a dream in which people were crying as they stood around a coffin in a room in the White House. President Lincoln, in his dream, asked the guard on duty who had died. The guard replied it was President Lincoln who had been killed by an assassin. President Lincoln told his friends about this dream. One month later, Lincoln was assassinated by John Wilkes Booth.

Main idea:

Dr. William James collected thousands of reports of people who believed they had ESP. Dr. Rhine, in the 1930s, set up experiments to test ESP. Dr. Montague Ullman recently set up a study to test his own telepathy powers on people who were sleeping.

Evaluation Criterion: Students' ability to write appropriate main ideas.

Extension and Integration:

READING: Students will be intrigued by the ESP passages and easily motivated to read about fascinating studies and reports. Suggested books:

BERGER, MELVIN. *The supernatural: from ESP to UFO's.* New York: John Day Company, 1977.
EDELSON, EDWARD. *The book of prophecy.* New York: Doubleday, 1974.
GELLER, URI. *My story.* New York: Praeger, 1975.
RHINE, LOUISA. *Mind over matter.* New York: Macmillan, 1970.

LISTENING: A number of books are available on testing ESP powers. Have students listen to these fairly simple sets of directions and test their own ESP abilities. Suggested books:

ATKINS, W. R. *ESP—your psychic powers and how to test them.* New York: Franklin Watts, 1980.
EBON, MARTIN. *Test your ESP.* New York: Thomas Y. Crowell, 1970.

SPEAKING: Based on their reading, students can devise a questionnaire on psychic ability and interview a number of people. Students can compile their results and perhaps even locate a local psychic. Students can also contact local police stations to find out if psychics have ever been used by the department to solve a crime.

THE INVERTED PYRAMID

Skill Area: Writing
Details

Background: Most news stories are written in an "inverted pyramid" format. That is, the important facts in a story—the *who, what, when, where,* and *why*—are found in the first paragraph or two of the story. Less important information follows in succeeding paragraphs. This style is followed for two reasons: (1) readers can get a quick summary of the news by reading only the first few paragraphs; and (2) editors with limited space can cut the end of the story without losing important facts.

Objectives: Given essential facts, pupils will write brief "newsy" paragraphs containing these facts.

Materials: Not necessary. News stories from newspapers might be useful if desired.

Activity: Explain the "inverted pyramid" concept of newswriting to the class and tell why the style is followed. Explain that a well-written news story will give you the essential information in a condensed form. The concept may be demonstrated using news stories from the local newspaper. (Make sure the stories are "hard" news and not feature or editorial material.) Pupils may also be invited to bring in newspaper clippings that illustrate this concept.

List a group of facts under the appropriate *who, what, when, where,* and *why* headings on the chalkboard; for example:

Who	The mayor and the city council
What	decided to raise taxes
Where	at City Hall
When	last night
Why	to build a new swimming pool.

The facts listed can be fictional or real, reflecting local items of interest. The facts could also relate to school or class news, or to books that pupils have read. Ask pupils to combine these facts into a single sentence or two short sentences. Encourage pupils to combine the items in different ways. Have pupils suggest other facts that can be combined using the inverted pyramid style.

Evaluation Criterion: Pupils' ability to produce paragraphs according to this newswriting style.

Extension and Integration:

READING: Have pupils read newspapers stories that illustrate the inverted pyramid style. Stories written with this concentrated style provide excellent material for literal comprehension exercises.

WRITING: After they have written the "lead" paragraph for a news story (using the inverted pyramid format), have pupils finish the story on their own. Encourage them to supply more information on each of the details presented in the first paragraph or two.

THE FRONT PAGE

Skill Area: Writing
Main Ideas and Details

Background: Writing a class/school newspaper generates a high degree of productivity and excitement on the part of students. Their writing has a real purpose. The following activity asks students to write newspaper articles using the main idea/detail framework.

Objective: The students, in groups, will investigate school events and write articles for a one-page newspaper.

Materials: Local newspapers—one per student.

Activity: At least a day in advance, ask students to bring in a local newspaper.

Say "Before you take your newspapers out of your desks, can you tell me what a reader usually finds on the front page?" List students' responses on the blackboard (headlines, date, pictures, and so forth).

Have students take out their newspapers, locate and explain the parts of the front page listed on the board. For example:

a. circle the date
b. underline the major headlines
c. box the index
d. place a check mark on the weather

Have students identify parts of the front page not previously listed.

For older students, an introduction to the three types of news: local, national, and international will be beneficial. Ask students to first examine each of these terms from a sports prospective: "Have any of you competed in a local swimming/tennis meet? What is the local competion? Do you know anyone who has competed at the national level? How many of you have watched the Olympics in which people compete in an international level?" Have students then draw parallels between the sports and news categories and locate headlines that cover local, national, and international news.

Once the students are familiar with the parts of the front page, suggest that they write the smallest newspaper in the world—a newspaper with only one page, the front page.

Divide the class into small groups, each responsible for finding a "school story." It may be helpful to have the class brainstorm on school events, such as, girls are trying out for the baseball team for the first time in the school's history; the fourth graders are going on a field trip to Salem; the principal's new detention policy.

When the groups have gathered their data through observation, interviews, and correspondence each group can compose its article. (Review concept of main idea/details presented on page 126.) Stress the importance of proofreading and editing drafts.

Groups can then exchange stories and act as editors, making necessary changes. When the articles are in final form, they can be read to the class, weighted in importance, and arranged accordingly on the front page.

Have the front page typed up (perhaps by older students taking a typing course) and distributed as widely as possible.

Evaluation Criterion: Students' ability to organize collected data into written articles.

Extension and Integration:

READING/SPEAKING/LISTENING: Group students so that at least two different newspapers are represented per group. Have students compare the front pages for headlines, pictures, number and content of stories covered, etc. Discuss their findings. A local reporter/editor can even be invited to the classroom to discuss the decision-making process and factors that affect the editor's selection of stories.

WRITING: Note-taking skills are of critical importance to a newspaper reporter. Students can be introduced to note-taking techniques and given opportunities to observe situations and record important data.

READING: Provide students with additional practice in finding main ideas by separating headlines from articles and asking students to then rematch them. Discuss how headlines are main ideas.

WHAT'S IN AN AD?

Skill Area: Writing
Reference Skills

Background: To write a classified ad, students must be able to distinguish between the essential and the nonessential, to focus on key ideas/words. The following activity introduces children to this succinct form of written expression as a prerequisite to the skill of note-taking.

Objective: Given two detailed, wordy advertisements, the students will rewrite the ads using more succinct language.

Materials: Classified ads (examples provided).

Activity: Say, "Suppose you owned a puppy that you had to sell because your family was moving into an apartment where dogs weren't allowed. How would you sell your dog?"

Discuss various responses, and conclude that most of the time people put ads in the newspaper to sell things. Hang the following ads on the board and have students read them.

```
Cockerspaniel, fluffy and adorable;
shots, paper-trained, great with kids.
$50.00  Call after 5:00.   393-1234
```

```
I want to sell a cockerspaniel.  He is
fluffy and adorable.  He has had his shots.
He is also trained to go to the bathroom
on paper.  He is a great puppy with kids.
You can buy him for just $50.  Please call
after 5:00 p.m.  My number is 393-1234.
```

Explain that it costs so much money per word to put an ad in the newspaper. Ask students which of the ads they would use if they had to pay for each word. Comment on why people use as few words as possible. Ask students what kind of words are in the short ad; explain they are key words.

Give students practice in reading advertisements.

Basset hound puppy; 10 months old; brown and white; female; all shots—$15.00. After 5:30. 555-8488	Free Golden Retriever to good home. Call after 4:00 P.M. 555-3456

How old is the puppy?
What color is the puppy?
Has she had her shots?
How much does the puppy cost?
What time can you call the owner?

What kind of dog is being sold?
Do you know how much the dog cost?
Can you call the owner during lunch?

Husky dog 6 yrs. old, male, well groomed, moving to apartment, must sell. Asking $100-150. 555-4576	Affectionate and playful, solid black Labrador pup, 10 wks. old, good watchdog. 555-4587

Is this a puppy?

If you have $50, can you buy this dog?

Do the owners take good care of the the dog?

Why is the dog being sold?

How can you find out what the dog will cost?

Why is the pup a good dog for children?

Do we know if it has had its shots?

What color is the pup?

Will the dog scare away robbers?

Students are now ready to write their own ads from the following lengthy versions:

My collie just had five puppies. The puppies have blonde and white coats. They look like Lassie. The puppies are 2 months old. There are two males, and three females. I will sell each puppy for $65. I will be home everyday after school at 3:00. My telephone number is 555-6243.

I would like to sell my brown and white hunting dog for $50. He has been trained by professionals at a training school and has hunted very successfully for the past three years. Because we are moving to the city I must part with a great hunting dog. Please call between 6:00 and 9:00. 555-1247.

Evaluation Criterion: Students' ability to rewrite ads in more succinct language.

Extension and Integration:

READING: Students may be unfamiliar with some of the dogs mentioned in the above activity. Encourage them to consult reference books for pictures/details about unfamiliar dogs.

READING: Introduce students to the classified ad section of the newspaper; explore various headings. Give students different situations, such as, "Pat wants to buy a 1972 white Porsche." Have them read the ads and locate one that addresses the buyer's needs. Students may have to be introduced to key vocabulary words/abbreviations to ensure successful reading.

WRITING: Create a For Sale bulletin board and have students in conjunction with their parents write ads for toys/items that they want to sell.

TWENTY YEARS FROM NOW.....

Skill Area: Writing
Making Predictions

Background: Making predictions as a high level cognitive skill that requires students to ponder existing conditions and circumstances and posit plausible outcomes. What better way to introduce this skill to students than by having them make personal predictions about the future.

Objective: The students will make predictions about five aspects of their lives 20 years from now.

Materials: Construction paper.

Activity: Have children find a comfortable place to sit, close their eyes, and think about the following:

> "Imagine yourself 20 years from now. That's right, you'll be *xx* years old. What will you look like then? (Pause, let students speak if they choose to.) Think about the clothes you'll be wearing (pause), your hairstyle. Can you see yourself (pause)?"
>
> "What job you will have? Will you be a police officer, a painter, a doctor, a telephone man or woman, a salesperson? Can you see yourself working?"
>
> "What kind of a car will you drive (pause)? Will it be a small sports car or a large family car? Can you see yourself driving your new car to work (pause)?"
>
> "What will you do for fun? Will you play tennis? Can you see yourself having fun? What are you doing (pause)? Won't it be fun to be *xx* years old?"

Have the children open their eyes. Explain that you have just had them make predictions about their futures, based on what they know about themselves. Give them a chance to share their imaginations and suggest that it might be fun for each student to make a booklet of his or her predictions. Each student can use two large pieces of construction paper, fold them in half and make a booklet containing six pages, one page for each of the following predictions:

- what they will look like;
- what their job will be;
- where they will live and with whom;
- what kind of car they will own;
- what they will do for fun.

On each page, the student will paste a magazine picture that depicts their prediction. Under the picture, the student will write predictions with an explanation.

Evaluation Criteria: Students' ability to make predictions about each of five aspects of their future lives.

Extension and Integration:

READING: Have friends pair up for this reading activity. Students can discover how well they know their friends by guessing what their friends' predictions are; for example, students can ask their friends what they think their job will be. After the friend guesses, the students can show their illustrations and read their predictions.

WRITING: Have students write a letter to their parents explaining their prediction booklet. In the letter students can ask parents to put the booklet in a safe place so when they are older they can find out if their predictions were correct.

READING: People who claim to be clairvoyant are in the business of making predictions. Students can read the predictions of famous psychics such as Jean Dixon and keep records of those that are confirmed or rejected.

WHAT'S GOING TO HAPPEN NOW?

Skill Area: Writing
Making Predictions

Background: Children and adults often make predictions about everyday happenings, from figuring out the ending of a mystery on T.V. to predicting outcomes of real-life events and crises. The following activity challenges students to think through situations and predict possible outcomes.

Objective: Given story-starters, the students will write story outcomes.

Materials: Comic strips; situation cards (examples provided).

Activity:

PREPARATION: Locate eight to ten comic strips with fairly predictable endings in newspapers. Cut off the last frame(s) that contains the comic strip's ending.

Tape one of the incomplete comic strips to the blackboard. (If you are using this activity with the whole class, you will need to enlarge the comic strip on the opaque projector.) Read and discuss each frame of this comic strip. Point out that the ending is missing. Ask students what they think will happen; ask them to make predictions.

Discuss predictions; students can vote for the best prediction. Tape the missing frame(s) and compare results. Have students react to author's ending. Stress that often there is no single correct answer, that a number of reasonable possibilities exist; the author chose the one she or he thought was best.

Divide the class into small groups. Present an incomplete comic strip to each group. Students can read the frames and write out their predictions. Hand each group the ending frame(s) and have them compare endings.

Explain that figuring out the ending of a comic strip is only one situation in which people predict outcomes. Ask students if they can think of other situations in which they figure out endings (predict outcomes), such as, predicting how a story or T.V. show will end, or looking at the sky and predicting the weather.

Ask students to predict the outcome(s) of the following real-life situation:

Ted and Richie are reading the directions on the fire alarm box in the principal's office. Richie accidently touches the wrong lever and sets off the fire alarm. What will happen?

Have students predict obvious outcomes. Discuss the importance of thinking about consequences of our actions before taking them.

Write the following situations on the blackboard:

"Class, we're going outside for a short recess but please be careful on the playground. Much of the playground is covered with ice," said the teacher. Pat and Joan rushed out of the classroom, put on their coats, and dashed out to the playground. "Hurry up," said Joan, "or we won't get a swing."

"Today, we're going to plant our corn seeds," said Mrs. Simonian. "Listen carefully to . . ." Mrs. Simonian stopped, looked at Peter and said, "Please stop talking so you can hear the directions." Mrs. Simonian started again "Listen carefully to the steps for planting . . ." but couldn't finish the sentence. Peter was still talking.

"Art is my favorite class," said Jeannette, as she took the lid off the bottle of red paint. "Art used be my favorite subject," said Marguerite, "but now, history is." Marguerite removed the lids from the yellow and blue paints. Jeannette dipped her

> brush into the red paint and made a big valentine. "Who's it for?" asked Marguerite. "My father," said Jeannette as she dipped her brush, which still had red paint on it, into the blue paint. As she started to write on the paper, she said "Oh, no."

Ask students to select one of the situations and write an ending. Remind them to think about various outcomes and select the most appropriate ones.

Evaluation Criterion: Students' ability to write stories that contain appropriate outcomes.

Extension and Integration:

READING/SPEAKING: Predicting outcomes is an excellent technique for keeping students in tune with current events. As national and international events unfold, student can obtain pertinent information and make predictions about future courses of action. To discover whether their predictions are confirmed, students must stay actively involved in current events.

SPEAKING: People in various occupations make predictions everyday. Have students brainstorm these occupations and the kinds of predictions being made, for example, scientists (predicting volcanic eruptions), gamblers (betting on horses, sports), fortunetellers, advertisers.

READING: Scientific experiments lend themselves beautifully to the skill of predicting outcomes. Experiments can be set up so that students are required to predict outcomes before engaging in the actual experiment. Feedback on their predictions, of course, is immediate.

STATE YOUR OPINION

Skill Area: Writing
Fact and Opinion

Background: An important dimension of critical thinking is the ability to distinguish fact from opinion. According to Pearson and Johnson (1978), "Distinguishing facts from opinion is not the kind of task that should be left to chance. It requires thoughtful guidance on your part as a teacher. Such guidance includes generous modeling, numerous examples and substantive feedback" (p. 139). The following activity reviews the distinction between fact and opinion and asks students to write opinions from factual information.

Objective: The students will write opinions from stated facts.

Materials: A short fact and opinion passage (example provided); a worksheet of facts (example provided).

Activity: Write the following message on the board and read it to the students:

> "I think that dogs are a nuisance," said Lynn. "Most of them shed their hair all around the house. They cost money to feed. They bark, and you have to give them baths. Dogs just aren't worth the trouble."

Make two columns on the board, the first labeled *FACTS,* and the second *OPINIONS.*

Ask students to relate how Lynn feels about having a dog. Write their response in the *OPINION* column and call their attention to the point that opinions are statements that people believe to be true but which can't be proven to be true. Explain that everyone is entitled to his or her opinion and should be allowed to express it.

Explain that facts, on the other hand, are statements that can be proven to be true (either through observation or records). Ask the students to identify the facts that Lynn used in forming her opinion. As students respond, ask them how they can prove their response is a fact. List facts under the appropriate column.

Ask how many students share Lynn's opinion. Have them explain why. Ask how many disagree with Lynn's opinion and why. Have them share their opinions about dogs. Responses can be recorded.

Write the following pairs of sentences on the board.

An apple is a fruit.	Apples taste better than oranges.
Every baseball game has a pitcher.	Baseball is a great sport.
No woman has ever been president of the U.S.	The next president should be a woman.

Have the students read these statements and decide which column contains facts and which contains opinions; have them explain why.

Hand out a worksheet which contains the following facts. Have students write an opinion about each fact.

FACTS	*YOUR OPINIONS*
1. McDonalds sells hamburgers.	
2. People use motorcycles to travel to work.	
3. Lions roam the jungles of Africa.	
4. School is a place where students learn.	

5. A touchdown in football earns that team 6 points.
6. February 14th is Valentine's Day.
7. There are many breeds of dogs.
8. There are a number of comedy shows on T.V.

Students can share their opinions about various facts; stress that since opinions aren't verifiable, a number of opinions about the same fact can exist.

Evaluation Criterion: Students' ability to write opinions about stated facts.

Extension and Integration:

READING: Travel brochures often provide students with an excellent opportunity for distinguishing fact from opinion. Students can read an advertisement, circle all the opinions, and underline all the facts.

The Happy Hotel contains *200* luxurious rooms, each with its own television and breath-taking view of the ocean.

SPEAKING: Encourage students to extend their understanding of fact and opinion to everyday crises. Students can be asked to report the facts of the incident observed and conclude with their opinion.

LISTENING/WRITING: After a discussion of a current event in the news, read an editorial on that topic, and ask students to identify the editor's opinions. Students can propose opposing views and write letters of rebuttal to the editor.

LANGUAGE ACTIVITIES

Language is the "stuff" of which language arts instruction is made. Language consists of the signals of speech—the sounds and the meaning elements and the syntax that allow us to send messages to another. In a classroom sense, language also consists of the conventions of writing—the letter combinations that represent the sounds and the grammatical relationships that make sentence meanings clear and the other mechanical devices that make written communication clear and effective. These are the foci of the activities that follow.

Language is rich in meaning. It contains all the elements that humans need to communicate their thoughts and emotions to one another. Within the classroom, one of the major aims of language study is to help pupils discover the power of the language they speak. This involves helping pupils to discover the richness of language, to find its multiple meanings, to study and come to appreciate its intricate and very useful structure, and to learn its enormous flexibility.

Classroom language arts instruction extends the study of language into writing. Written language preserves ideas over time and space. Writing involves spelling, the skill that enables children to attach the appropriate letters to the sounds of the words they want to use. It involves handwriting so that their thoughts can be interpreted by others. It involves written conventions like punctuation and capitalization, so that what they write will be both linguistically and socially acceptable. As an area of instruction, it involves the full range of skills that pupils need to effectively convey their thoughts in written form.

There are practical pay-offs to the study of spoken and written language. Children who possess a sizable vocabulary and who know how to use this vocabulary appropriately will be judged accordingly. The pupil who knows how to select just the right word to express the idea that he/she has will communicate more clearly and effectively in speech and writing. Similarly, the conventional mechanical standards—such as using the proper grammatical form or using the correct punctuation—are often powerful determinants of the effectiveness of one's writing.

But beyond practical concerns, there is an important affective side to the study of language. It's unfortunate when creative ideas are sacrificed to mechanical accuracy or when pupils come to profess that they "hate English" as a result of hours of overanalysis. Studying language can enhance pupils' respect and appreciation for their mother tongue. While parts of speech and periods and commas and spelling and handwriting are all important and necessary dimensions of the language arts, the study of such matters should not detract from the fact that language is alive and well in the minds and mouths of each pupil in every classroom. Making language alive is the ultimate end of language instruction in the classroom.

ALLITERATIVE ADJECTIVES

Skill Area: Language
Vocabulary

Background: *Alliteration* is a literary device that begins two or more of matched words with the same beginning sounds. Alliteration is used in literature to convey effective images. Who cannot envisage Kipling's "great, gray-green greasy Limpopo River?" Alliteration can be used in the classroom for auditory awareness, for vocabulary development, and for just plain language fun.

Objective: Given a list of nouns, the students will supply alliterative descriptive words for each noun on the list.

Materials: Chalkboard and/or overhead transparencies. For small group work, individual copies of lists may also be prepared for pupil use.

Activity: Write a list of the names of animals on the chalkboard each beginning with a different letter of the alphabet. For example:

alligator	hippopotamus	penguin
baboon	iguana	quail
cat	jackal	rabbit
donkey	kangaroo	seal
elephant	lion	turtle

Explain that alliteration is the process of using two related words that begin with the same sound. Ask a student to suggest a word beginning with the letter "a" to describe or tell more about *alligator* (*amazing alligator, astounding alligator, aggravating alligator,* and so forth). Follow the same procedure with the next two or three words on the list before allowing students to work on their own. Compile a complete list of student responses.

The activity can be done either in large groups (with whole class input to the teacher copying dictated responses) or in small groups (with one student working as a secretary).

Either on their own or with the help of a picture dictionary, children can compile other lists of words in various categories—people's occupations *(the alert astronaut),* fruits and vegetables *(the tasty tomato),* or sports expressions *(a tremendous touchdown).* Students might also string two or more alliterative modifiers together—*the amazingly amenable aardvark.*

Evaluation Criterion: Students' ability to produce a variety of interesting alliterative modifiers.

Extension and Integration:

LANGUAGE: This activity necessarily lends itself to manipulating parts of speech, so adjective-noun relationships may be part of, or a follow-up to, the activity; also, with expressions such as the *amazingly amenable aardvark,* the role of the adverb as an adjective modifier can be taught.

WRITING: When a list of alliterative expressions has been compiled, students can construct sentences using the expressions; for example, *The quizzical quail tried to catch the flying fish.* The list might also be used to construct a class story—possible title: *The Zany Zoo.*

SPEAKING: Pupils can make facial expressions to communicate what their alliterative animal looks like. They might also act out what might happen when one alliterative animal meets another.

HANDWRITING: Here pupils use the alliterative pairs for handwriting practice on appropriate letters of the alphabet.

EDGE OR KILL

Skill Area: Language
Vocabulary

Background: Children's language is more effective when their sentences "come alive." One proven way of enlivening speech and writing is to avoid the use of overworked expressions—expressions that are used time and time again. This activity aims to have students use a variety of vibrant synonyms for overused verbs.

Objective: When presented with an overused verb, the students will suggest a list of more interesting synonyms for the verb.

Materials: A list of sports scores from the newspaper.

Activity: Bring a list of scores clipped from the sports section of the newspaper. The list can be professional baseball scores, college football scores, the scores of local high school contests, or any list in which students may be interested. Ask students to imagine that you are a sports announcer and read the list of scores using only the verb *beat* ("Boston beat New York 4–2, San Diego beat Pittsburg 7–1, Chicago beat Detroit 4–0, . . .") See if students notice the repetition of the word *beat,* and ask them to suggest the effect of overusing this word. Have students suggest synonyms, for example: *defeated, edged, killed, clobbered, squeezed by, trounced,* etc. Write these synonyms on the chalkboard as they are suggested. Have a student reread the list, using the synonyms.

Write other typically overused verbs on the board, such as *talked, ran, came.* Divide the class into groups and ask each group to suggest a list of synonyms for these words. Have students write or dictate sentences using these words. A more specific context can be provided for this group activity by giving each group a sports story and having them supply synonyms within the context of the story; for example:

> "The halfback
> ran down the field. . . .
> sprinted down the field. . . .
> dashed down the field. . . .
> rambled down the field, etc."

Evaluation Criterion: Students' ability to produce lists of effective synonyms.

Extension and Integration:

LISTENING: Dictate sentences in which the meaning of the verb does not fit the context of the sentence, for example: "New York killed Los Angeles 1–0, Atlanta edged Baltimore 14–2, etc." Have students identify the semantic inconsistency in the sentences.

READING: Have students locate or suggest alternatives for overused words in material that they read.

WRITING: Keep an ongoing record of synonym lists that children can use in their writing.

CHAIRMAN OR CHAIRPERSON

Skill Area: Language
Vocabulary .

Background: Feminism has heightened our consciousness regarding sexism in language, and there has been a concerted effort to avoid sexist terms. Thus, *chairman* has now become *chairperson, policeman* has become *police officer,* and other male-oriented terms are being changed. The following activity is designed to alert students to these changes in our language.

Objective: The students will suggest nonsexist terms in place of "male-oriented" terms.

Materials: None.

Activity: Write the words *chairman, policeman,* and *fireman* on the chalkboard. Call attention to the *-man* as the final element in these words. Explain that *-man* has long been used to indicate these roles because traditionally only men served in these roles. However, since these roles are changing to include more and more women, the terms to describe these roles are also changing. Ask students to suggest terms to describe these roles that would not include the term *-men.* See if they can suggest terms like *chairperson, police officer, firefighter.*

On the chalkboard or on a Ditto master, make a list of terms such as the following:

first baseman	newsman	mailman	bat boy
doorman	anchorman	bus boy	delivery man
salesman	cowboy	snowman	mankind

Ask students to suggest "nonsexist equivalent terms" for these words. Tell students that they are not allowed merely to suggest "person" in place of "man" or "boy." Students can work either individually or in pairs. When the class has finished making the lists, have students compare terms.

Evaluation Criterion: Students' completed list of alternative terms.

Extension and Integration:

WRITING: Students can write sentences using the alternative terms.

HANDWRITING: Students can practice their handwriting by copying the lists that are suggested.

LISTENING: Students can be alerted to listen for these nonsexist terms in the language they hear at home or on television.

HOMONYM TIC-TAC-TOE

Skill Area: Language
Vocabulary

Background: *Homonyms* or *homophones*—words that are pronounced the same, but have different meanings and spellings—can often be troublesome for children. Such words are easily confused and often misused in written language. The following activity introduces students to the concept of homonyms and asks them to identify homonyms appropriate to various sentence contexts.

Objective: Given sentences containing homonyms, the student will write the homonym appropriate to the context of the sentence.

Materials: Index cards; list of homonyms (examples provided); list of sentences containing homonyms (examples provided).

Activity: Ask students to write the following sentence on a piece of paper:

See the flea flee to the sea.

Have students compare results with a neighbor. Ask students what was unusual about the sentence. Ask if anyone knows what you call two words that sound the same but are spelled differently; write *flee, flea* and *see, sea* on the board. Introduce the term *homonym.*

From the following list of homonyms, write one homonym per index card: | deer | | dear | ; select pairs appropriate to students' grade level.

cents—sense	principle—principal	beach—beech
heard—herd	meat—meet	not—knot
son—sun	flour—flower	pair—pare
pain—pane	sale—sail	bear—bare

toe—tow	pale—pail	our—hour
beet—beat	eight—ate	bore—boar
would—wood	witch—which	

Students can review common homonyms by playing the following match-up game:

- Pass out an index card to each student.
- Have one student stand up and read her or his word; ask the student in the audience who has the same word, spelled differently, to also stand up.
- Ask the audience to explain the difference between the homonyms and use the words in sentences.
- Repeat procedure for remaining words.

To illustrate the importance of knowing when to use which homonym, play Homonym Tic-Tac-Toe. Divide the group into two teams. Draw a Tic-Tac-Toe diagram on the board. Read each of the following sentences to the group and have each student write the word that is a homonym on a piece of paper as quickly as possible. The first person to hold up the correct homonym places an X or an O on the Tic-Tac-Toe for their team. The game ends when one team has three Xs or Os horizontally, vertically, or diagonally. Sample sentences:

1. "My *son* is three years old. Spell *son*."
2. "That dog is for *sale*. Spell *sale*."
3. "*Write* your name. Spell *write*."
4. "I *won* the game. Spell *won*."
5. "You look *pale*. Spell *pale*."
6. "Cook the *meat*. Spell *meat*."
7. "He *ate* too much. Spell *ate*."
8. "They *heard* the robbers. Spell *heard*."
9. "Bake cakes with *flour*. Spell *flour*."
10. "The *tow* truck moved our car. Spell *tow*."

Older students can be challenged not only to write the designated word in each of the above sentences, but also to supply its homonym. For example, the answer to number 3 would be *write - right*.

Evaluation Criterion: Students' ability to write the homonym appropriate to the sentence context.

Extension and Integration:

LISTENING: Children will enjoy listening to any of the following books in which authors play with homonyms:

SAGE, MICHAEL. *If you talked to a boar.* Philadelphia: Lippincott, 1960.
VAN GELDER, ROSALIND. *Monkeys have tails.* New York: McKay, 1961.
WHITE, MARY. *Twin words.* New York: Abingdon, 1961.

SPELLING: Create a Homonym Word-Find. List words and have students find and circle corresponding homonyms in the word-find box.

meat

too

sew

M			
E			
E		S	
T	W	O	

READING: The selection of the correct homonym depends upon the context of the sentence. Students can be given sentences in which they are to use context clues to choose the correct word:

Bread is on _____ this week.
        (sale, sail)

SAY THAT WORD AGAIN

Skill Area: Language
Vocabulary

Background: The English language is as flexible as it is rich. Common words often have many different meanings. Knowing the range of meanings that a word has can enhance a child's language power.

Objective: The students will think of as many meanings as possible for common words.

Materials: Index Cards.

Activity: Write the simple word *RUN* on the chalkboard. Ask students to think of as many meanings as they can for this word. List each meaning that the class suggests. (The number of meanings that the group suggests will vary according to the grade level and language background of the children. Some meanings for *run* include: to move fast, to seek political office, a score in baseball, to operate (a machine), to flow (as water), a tear (as in your stocking). There are actually over a hundred meanings and uses of the word. As students suggest a meaning, have them use the word in a sentence that illustrates the meaning.

On index cards or small slips of paper, write other common words that have a number of different meanings: for example:

right (correct; direction; immediate, as in right on time; privilege; etc.)
field (farm area; position in baseball; area of battle; etc.)
hit (strike; popular song; a baseball term; etc.)
well (hole in the ground; good feeling; thoroughly; etc.)
trip (journey; stumble; set free; etc.)

Divide the class into groups of five students. Allow each group to choose a word card and think of as many different meanings as they can for the word on the card. Place a time limit on the groups. When each group has listed as many meanings for a word as they can, the group's list should be read to the whole class and additional meanings should be added by other groups. Any time a meaning is suggested, the word should be used in a sentence to illustrate the meaning.

Evaluation Criterion: Number of meanings students can suggest for each word.

Extension and Integration:

LANGUAGE: When students "run out of steam" in suggesting meanings for words, they may be allowed to consult a dictionary to make word cards to be used by other groups.

LANGUAGE: As students in one group use the word in a sentence, other groups can identify the part of speech of that word; for example:

You have the *right* to remain silent. (noun)
Raise your *right* hand. (adjective)
The water came *right* up to the back door. (adverb)

WRITING: Students can write sentences using the word several different times with different meanings in the same sentence; for example:

Darryl raised his *right* hand *right* away when he got the *right* answer.

UNDERSTANDING IDIOMS

Skill Area: Language
Vocabulary

Background: Idioms, which abound in our language, can be a source of confusion for children since they require an understanding of figurative language. The following activity provides students with an opportunity to explore idiomatic expressions and determine how their figurative meanings evolved from the literal use of the words.

Objective: Given idiomatic expressions, the students will illustrate the idioms in both their literal and figurative meanings.

Materials: Story containing idioms (example provided); idioms (list provided); index cards; construction paper.

Activity: Pass out copies of the following script to students:

SETTING:

A surprise party at the Cunningham House for Mr. Cunningham. Guests are shooting the breeze, waiting for the arrival of Mr. C. Doorbell rings.

FONZI: (Hits the lights) Hey, cool it! Let's get this show on the road. (Opens door) Richie, where's Mr. C.? You were suppose to unload him here at 7:00.

RICHIE: (Ready to explode) I'm going to wring somebody's neck. I've just been on a wild goose chase and the goose is nowhere to be found.

FONZI: (Turning to the guests) OK, who blew it?

JOANIE: Oh, it was an accident. Dad knows about the party, but he promised . . .

MR. C.: (Sauntering downstairs) Had you going, didn't I?

Have students, taking parts, read the script. Ask students to identify expressions made popular by Fonzi; record them on board. Discuss the literal and figurative meaning of each expression; explain the term *idiom*. Have students return to the script and circle as many idiomatic expressions as they can find. Discuss literal and figurative meanings.

Have students team up with a partner. Pass out construction paper to each team and an index card which contains an idiom. Instruct students to illustrate the literal meaning of the idiom on one side of the construction paper and the figurative on the other. Each team then shares their illustrations with the class and explains how they think the figurative meaning evolved from the literal.

It's
raining
cats and dogs

It's
raining
cats and dogs

The following list of idioms may be helpful:

break the ice	button up your lips	in hot water
take the bull by the horns	split hairs	on his high horse
stick out my neck	can't hold a candle to	hang in there
cut him down	barking up the wrong tree	flipped his lid
sleep like a log	hang it up	walking on thin ice
spic and span	climbing the walls	up in the air
your goose is cooked	at the end of your rope	

Evaluation Criterion: Students' ability to illustrate the literal and figurative meanings of idioms.

Extension and Integration:

READING: Students uncertain as to the figurative meanings of some idioms can consult: Funk, Charles. *Heavens to Betsy and other curious sayings.* New York: Harper & Row, 1955.

WRITING: Each generation spawns its own stock of idioms; youngsters enjoy using expressions unfamiliar to adults—secret language. Have students compile a book of current idiomatic expressions complete with literal and figurative illustrations.

LANGUAGE: Students can categorize idiomatic expressions according to figurative meanings, for example:

> *Be careful.*
> Walk on thin ice.
> Don't stick out your neck.
> Don't go out on a limb.
> Tread slowly.

PREPOSITION PARADE

Skill Area: Language: Parts of Speech

Background: Prepositions constitute a relatively small but very useful group of words in our language. Students need not only learn to identify prepositions as a part of speech but also to use prepositional phrases to make their descriptive writing more effective.

Objective: Students will identify and define the preposition as a part of speech.

Materials: A list of sentences or an article.

Activity: Write the following list of common prepositions on the chalkboard, on a chart, or on an overhead transparency:

above	below	from	past
around	beside	in	through
among	between	into	to
at	beyond	of	toward
across	by	off	under
before	during	on	with
behind	for	over	without

Have the class read the list or have one student read the list as another points to the words being read. Then write the following sentence for the class to read:

Over the hills and *through* the woods *to* grandmother's house we go.

Explain that the underlined words are *prepositions,* little words that show relationships in sentences. Examine the sentence to see how the underlined words show the relationship of the nouns *hills, woods,* and *house* to the other words in the sentence. These prepositions show a "place" relationship. Other prepositions can show a "time" relationship *(during, after, before)* and others can show a "manner" relationship *(with, for, like).* Students should also learn that a preposition is always followed by a noun or a pronoun. When not followed by a noun or a pronoun, the words above may be used as adverbs; for example:

The cat ran *up* the stairs. (preposition)
Then it looked *up.* (adverb)

Give students a writing sample—a list of sentences or an article from a newspaper or children's magazine—and have them circle all the prepositions they find. This activity can be done by pupils working individually or in small groups.

Using the list, have students dictate other prepositional phrases; for example:

around the corner	across the street	over your head
under the table	at lunch	behind him
in the box	before school	off the grass

This activity can be done in small groups. After the list of prepositions has been introduced and shared with the class, divide the students into groups of three to five. Give groups timed practice to see how many prepositional phrases they can think of. (They may use a tape recorder or write a list to keep a record.)

Evaluation Criteria: Students' abilities to identify prepositions and dictate prepositional phrases.

Extension and Integration:

LISTENING: As you read a story, have students listen carefully for prepositions. Have students raise their hand each time they hear one read.

READING: Have students call attention to prepositional phrases that they encounter in their basal reader or other classroom reading experiences.

READING: Make a list of prepositional phrases on cards and have students use these cards for phrase reading as part of oral reading practice.

WRITING: Demonstrate the importance of prepositions in precise writing. Show how the direction "Draw a circle over the triangle" can mean:

Have students write their own directions using prepositional phrases.

ALPHABETICAL ORDER

Skill Area: Language
Alphabetizing

Background: Successful use of dictionaries, indexes, and telephone directories requires a knowledge of alphabetization. In the following activity, students are asked to create their own self-correcting game by brainstorming items for popular categories and alphabetizing the items accordingly.

Objective: Given the various categories, the students will list items for the categories and alphabetize the items accordingly.

Materials: Magazines; a worksheet divided into six sections (example provided); glue or stapler.

Activity: Review the skill of alphabetizing by having students brainstorm their favorite desserts; list responses on the board. Divide the class into groups. Supply each group with a piece of chart paper and a magic marker. Have each group alphabetize the desserts listed on the board. (If the list contains two or more desserts having the same initial letter or letters, such as cake and candy, it would be advisable to review the appropriate procedure for alphabetizing such words before the group started.) Tape each list on the board so that students can compare results.

After the review, explain to the students that they are going to make an alphabet game. The steps involved in making the game are as follows:

1. List a number of categories on the board (sports, colors, animals, cars).
2. Ask each student to choose a category and on a piece of scrap paper, list six items that belong to that category. (For older students, you may ask them to think up six items all starting with the same letters.) Encourage students to check their spelling in the dictionary. Then have students alphabetize their six items.
3. Pass out a worksheet that has been divided into six equal sections, marked by dotted lines. Have the students write each item in a section of the worksheet in alphabetical order. A student who chooses the sports category might have a worksheet that looks like this:

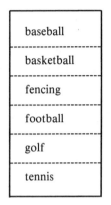

4. Using magazines, have each student cut out a picture (preferably one that represents their category) that approximates the size of the worksheet (8½" x 11"). Students can trim the magazine picture so that it is congruent with the worksheet.
5. Have students glue or staple the magazine picture to the *blank* side of one worksheet so that when completed, one side of the worksheet has six items in alphabetical order and the other side has a magazine picture glued to it.
6. Have students then cut along the dotted lines, finishing with six word cards.
7. Each student then scrambles the six word cards and places them into an envelope; the student can write the category on the envelope.
8. The students exchange envelopes and alphabetize the six word cards. Once the words are alphabetized, the student can check his or her work by flipping over each word card in its place. If the picture is complete, the student has alphabetized correctly. If parts of the picture are out of sequence, the student must turn over all the cards and re-alphabetize the six words.
9. Laminating the word cards in each envelope will enhance the durability of the games.

Evaluation Criteria: Students' ability to generate items for a category and alphabetize them.

Extension and Integration:

LISTENING/SPEAKING: Should the self-correcting device become a temptation for some students, it may be advisable to discuss the role of cheating in this activity. One way to address this issue is to read the following incident to the class:

> Brian and his partner had just exchanged envelopes. Brian was working carefully to put his words in alphabetical order. He had just finished alphabetizing his fourth word, when his partner said "I'm done. Boy, are you a slow poke!" and left to exchange envelopes with another student.
>
> Brian was upset. He quickly turned over the word cards and looking at the picture pieces, he arranged the picture quickly. He then exchanged his envelope with another student. This time he didn't even look at the words, he just put the picture pieces in order and said to his partner, "Boy, are you slow. I'm done."

Discuss what happened in the story with the class: "Why did Brian cheat? What did he learn during the lesson? How will he do on the alphabetizing test?"

SPEAKING: The category envelopes lend themselves beautifully to creative dramatics. Each student can pick an envelope and tell the class his or her category. The student then takes out a word card, reads it to himself, and acts out the word. The group must guess what the word is.

WRITING/SPEAKING: Supply students with six index cards. Have students take their category envelope and write a riddle (one per index card) for the six items in the envelope, that is, for the word card *airplane* the student writes the following riddle on an index card:

I have wings.
I carry people.
I have a motor.

Students then scramble the word cards and the riddle cards, and exchange envelopes with a partner. The partner matches each riddle to the appropriate word card.

PLEASE DON'T BE OBSTREPEROUS

Skill Area: Language
Dictionary

Background: The dictionary contains definitions for every word in our language. Very often, however, children will guess at the meaning of an unfamiliar word rather than taking time to check the definition of the word in a dictionary. The following activity involves students in guessing the meaning of words, but then requires them to confirm their guesses by using the dictionary.

Objective: The students will guess the definition of an unfamiliar word and then confirm their guess by checking the meaning of the word in the dictionary.

Materials: Word sheets with new vocabulary words.

Activity: Write the word *obstreperous* (or another word that students would be unlikely to know) on the chalkboard. Ask if anyone knows the meaning of this word and write students' responses on the board. Include one or two "guesses" of your own, one of which is correct (*noisy* or *unruly*). When four or five suggested meanings have been written on the board, have students "vote" on the most likely correct meaning. Then have them check the dictionary to confirm their guesses. This can be repeated once or twice as a whole-class activity.

Divide the students into groups of three or five. Give each group a list of new words and a stack of blank index cards. Students write a new word on each card. Then, each student writes one guess of the meaning of the word on the card. The group can then vote on the meaning they think is correct. When all guesses have been made, the cards are collected and passed to the next group. That group has the job of checking the dictionary for the meaning of the new word. The group that has the most correct guesses is declared winner.

When scores have been tallied, the definitions may be written on the back of each index card for later review.

Evaluation Criterion: Students' ability to find new word meanings in the dictionary.

Extension and Integration:

READING: For practice in context clues, each of the new words can be placed in a sentence with context clues to help students determine the meaning of the word; for example:

The minute the teacher left the room, the class became *obstreperous*.

Students then use context instead of, or in addition to, the dictionary in determining the meaning of the unknown words. When using this activity make sure sentences contain enough context for the student to figure out the meaning of the word. A sentence like, "He was an *obstreperous* person" does not contain any clues as to what the word might mean.

READING: This activity can be used as a prereading activity in a reading group as a means of introducing new words in a story.

WRITING: Since words take on full meaning as they are used in sentences, students can write or dictate sentences using the new words. This might be planned for review several days after the words have been introduced.

DICTIONARY JIGSAW

Skill Area: Language
Dictionary

Background: An important aspect of teaching dictionary skills is to help pupils develop a working knowledge of the major components of a dictionary entry. This activity allows pupils to develop this knowledge through the use of a puzzle.

Objective: Given an exercise with different puzzle formats, the students will supply pertinent information missing from the puzzle.

Materials: Teacher-made dictionary puzzles; activity sheet.

Activity: For several new vocabulary words, construct cardboard or oak tag "jigsaw puzzles" containing the word respelled in syllables, the phonetic spelling, the part of speech, and the more common definitions of the word. For example:

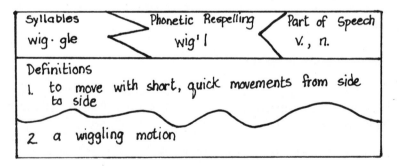

Cut out the puzzle pieces.

To introduce the activity, draw a puzzle on the chalkboard and explain what is contained in each puzzle "piece." Explain that taking the entry apart often makes it easier to determine what information is included. The activity can be carried out with the puzzles themselves or with activity sheets with puzzles drawn thereon.

With the puzzles themselves, break pieces apart and put puzzles for five words in a large envelope. Divide the class into groups and have groups race to reconstruct the puzzles. Review components with a quick verbal quiz with questions about the puzzle words; for example: "How many syllables are in the word *information?*" or "What part of speech is the word *proponent?*" Students should consult their puzzles to answer these questions.

With activity sheets, prepare exercise with five puzzle formats, with one "piece" of each puzzle filled in. Ask students to use their dictionaries to complete the rest of the puzzle. This exercise can be done competitively in small groups or by students working independently.

Evaluation Criteria: Students' abilities to use the dictionary to assemble puzzles and/or to complete exercise on activity sheets.

Extension and Integration:

LANGUAGE: For review of vocabulary, pupils can make up their own puzzles for use with other pupils. They should be warned to include only the two or three most common definitions of the words they use.

WRITING: Students can write sentences illustrating the different meanings of the puzzle words, or sentences using the word as the different parts of speech indicated in the dictionary entry.

SPELLING: The activity can be adapted to focus pupils' attention on comparing the phonetic respelling with the actual spelling of the word, thus reinforcing the correct spelling of the word.

SPELLING ON THE MOVE

Skill Area: Language
Spelling

Background: Spelling instruction in most classrooms is typically determined by the commercial spelling program in use. Since continual review and reinforcement plays a major role in spelling instruction, students should engage in various spelling activities before the final post-testing. The spelling games suggested below can be used to supplement the activities of the commercial spelling program and hopefully motivate students to master their spelling words.

Objective: Through action spelling games, the students will review their spelling words and demonstrate mastery.

Materials: Index cards; string.

Activity: Using the students' weekly spelling list from any of the commercial spelling programs, a variety of action games can be played. Before starting any games, encourage students to study their words according to their spelling program's word study guide for a 10-minute period. Suggested games:

HEADS UP: Write the list of spelling words on the board. Have students read and spell each word in unison. Choose one student to come up to the board. Have all other students put their heads on their desks and close their eyes. The student at the board then erases one word from the list and says "Heads Up." The first student to identify the missing word raises his or her hand and goes to the board to write the missing word in its place. If the word is spelled correctly, the student gets a chance to erase another word (after heads are down); if the word is spelled incorrectly, the original student gets another chance.

HANG IT UP: String a clothesline across one wall of the classroom. Attach seven or eight clothespins on each end of the line. Take each word on the spelling list and using index cards, spell out each word using one card per letter: | S | | P | | E | | L | | L | Since two teams will be playing simultaneously, make two sets of identical cards for each word. (Students, of course, can be involved in the preparation of this activity; stress importance of good handwriting.) Scramble the letters of each word and clip the pile together; repeat for all remaining words.

Divide the group into two teams (each group having a range of spelling abilities). Instruct the first student on each team to listen to the word given by the teacher, take the top pile of cards, unscramble the letters as quickly as possible, and hang them on the line in the correct order.

Teams can check to see if the two spellings match. If the word is spelled correctly, each team gets 5 points; in addition, the student who finished first gets an extra 5 points. The team with the most points wins.

REACH THE PEAK: Draw the following illustration on the board or on a chart.

Divide the group into two teams. Assign a captain from each team to stand on either side of the "mountain."

Pass out scrap paper to each student. Say a word from their weekly spelling list and have *each* student write the word down on a piece of scrap paper. When all pencils are down, show the correct spelling and have students pass in their responses (do not allow any changes to be made in words).

Examine each member's spelling of the word; for every correct response have the team captain move the mountain climber 1,000 feet up the mountain. Therefore the more children who spell the word correctly, the higher their team climbs on the mountain. Repeat this procedure with the other team.

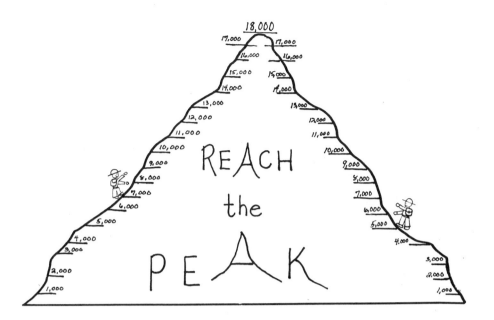

Say another spelling word and repeat above process. The team to reach the mountain peak first wins.

At the end of the week, post-test students to determine mastery of spelling words.

Evaluation Criterion: Students' ability to spell words correctly.

Extension and Integration:

SPEAKING: Students can choose words from their spelling list and act them out for the group. The first student in the audience to guess the word must raise his or her hand and then spell the word. If correct, that student gets to act out another word.

LANGUAGE: An excellent activity for expanding students' vocabularies is to take various root words from their spelling list and have students build a family tree of related words by attaching affixes to the root words. (See illustration on following page.)

LISTENING/SPELLING: Write a story that contains many of the weekly spelling words. Read the story and have students raise their hands when they hear a spelling word. Stop the story and have the whole class spell the word in unison.

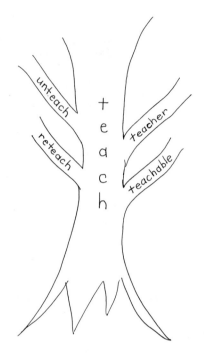

PERSONAL SPELLING WORDS

Skill Area: Language Spelling

Background: Commercial spelling programs cannot possibly meet the specific spelling needs of each and every child. One effective strategy for dealing with a range of spelling needs is to encourage children to identify their own spelling errors and allow them to periodically focus on a personal list of troublesome words.

Objective: The students will devise a personal list of troublesome words from their writing samples and, after a period of study, will demonstrate mastery of these words.

Materials: Writing samples for each student.

Activity: Write the following sentence on the board and read it to the class:

My friend said "Come and see my pet leopard anytime."

Ask students to reread the sentence silently and count the number of words that contain the short "e" sound. Circle the five words (fr*ie*nd, s*ai*d, p*e*t, l*eo*pard and *a*nytime) and underline the letters making the short "e" sound.

Discuss the fact that English can be a tricky language, that very often one sound can be written with a number of different letters, making our job as spellers a difficult one.

Return unedited writing samples (one or two) to each student. Have students team up with a partner and analyze their writing samples together for spelling errors. Each student can compile a list of personally troublesome spelling words. Students can study their spelling words, play spelling games, and quiz each other to assess progress.

The students' personal spelling lists can be collected and examined to discover words that are troublesome to a number of students in the classroom. A spelling chart can be created which contains the troublesome words spelled first phonetically, then accurately; for example:

SOUND SPELLING	PROPER SPELLING
becoz	because
cot	caught

This chart, posted in the classroom, allows students who can't remember the spelling of a troublesome word to look it up phonetically on the chart and find its proper spelling. Once students locate the same word a few times, they will begin to recall the proper spelling on their own.

Evaluation Criteria: Students' ability to examine writing samples, select troublesome words, and demonstrate mastery of these spelling words.

Extension and Integration:

SPELLING: The chart suggested in the above activity is a spinoff from Krensky and Linfield's, *The Bad Speller's Dictionary*. Purchasing copies of this inexpensive dictionary for students will provide them with a more extensive list of commonly mispelled words.

SPELLING: Encourage students to develop mnemonic devices for remembering the spelling of troublesome words; for example, to recall the "r" in the second syllable of February, students can learn to remember that February is a very cold month and "brrr" is the sound we make for cold; students can remember to check for the *br* in their spelling of February.

LISTENING: Address the issue of why many words in English aren't spelled phonetically by introducing them to the origins of the English language through the following books:

ADELSON, LEONE. *Dandelions don't bite.* New York: Pantheon, 1972.
DAVIDSON, JESSICA. *Is that mother in the bottle?* New York: Franklin Watts, 1972.
McCORMACK, JOANN. *The story of our language.* Columbus: Charles E. Merrill, 1967.

FOOD WORDS

Skill Area: Language
Spelling

Background: Teachers can effectively broaden the scope of their spelling programs by periodically substituting the program's spelling list with a thematic spelling list, a list of words that focus on a pertinent theme. For example, if students are studying about nutrition, the week's spelling list could be comprised of food words. Thus spelling is integrated into other curricular areas (science, social studies) and students are encouraged to use their spelling words in unit projects.

Objective: Through a variety of spelling games and activities, the students will demonstrate mastery of words on the thematic spelling list.

Materials: Thematic spelling list (example provided); various spelling games/activities (examples provided).

Activity: Choose a theme from which a list of spelling words (appropriate to age, ability of group) can be generated; for example, the theme *food* lends itself easily to the following list:

Pizza, pancakes, apple pie, spaghetti, tuna fish, hamburger, French fries . . .

Working in partners, students can pre-test each other to ascertain the words on which each student needs to concentrate. Encourage students to study their spelling words according to the word study guide in their regular spelling program. Present students with a variety of spelling games and activities to provide the reinforcement necessary for mastery. Suggested spelling activities follow:

1. Crossword puzzles: The one-to-one correspondence between the letters and the boxes in a crossword puzzle provides a helpful visual aid for students learning to spell new words. Crossword puzzles can be designed around the theme words.

2. Riddles: Have students read riddles built around the spelling words, such as:
   > You eat me with a fork, but I won't stay on your fork unless you twirl me round and round.
   >
   > <u>(Spaghetti)</u>

   Next, have them write the spelling word from memory.

3. Dictation: Students, working in pairs, can each select five favorite food words and devise sentences for each word. Students can take turns dictating their sentences to each other and compare results.

4. Spelling check: Encourage students, working with partners to frequently check on their spelling progress. Have students cut out pictures of the food words on their spelling list. On the back of each picture, students can write the spelling word. One student can then hold up the pictures while his or her partner spells the food words, and then they can exchange roles. Encourage students to chart their daily progress with the spelling words, keeping a record of words mastered.

5. Menus: Students can use the food pictures to design a lunch menu for 5 school-days. The words on the menu must be spelled from memory.

At the end of the week, students can post-test each other to determine how well the theme words were mastered.

Evaluation Criterion: Students' ability to master thematic spelling words.

Extension and Integration:

WRITING: While the "Friday" spelling test is a valid way to measure students' ability to retain a specified set of words, accurate usage of these words in context is just as critical. Students can be given creative writing assignments around the theme words; for example:

> You are a waiter/waitress in a restaurant. The tallest, skinniest man you have ever seen walks in and sits at one of your tables. He tells you he hasn't eaten in one week! Write a story about what he orders and how he eats his food.

READING/WRITING: Ideally, thematic word lists should be derived from units of study in other areas of the curriculum. Thus, if students were participating in a health unit on nutrition, the food words generated in the above activity would be very appropriate and relevant. Students would be reading books, watching films, doing experiments—activities packed with their spelling words. Most units require written projects which would provide the practical application for their spelling words.

SPELLING: Have students brainstorm a list of new spelling words around a more specific food theme: Foods that kids hate to eat.

LEARNING CURSIVE

Skill Area: Language
Handwriting

Background: Young school-age children are usually anxious to learn cursive writing. Mastery of the cursive style makes them feel like "big shots" because they can then "write like grown-ups." The following activity puts the learning and practice of cursive writing into a functional purpose.

Objective: Pupils will write personal letters to parents or other adults, using cursive handwriting.

Materials: Pencil and paper. A chart showing the standard personal letter format might also be needed if you want children to use the formal letter form.

Activity: Tell pupils that you're going to give them a chance to "show off." Tell them that they will write letters to any adult they choose, using a cursive style to show that they, too, can write like an adult.

Review the purpose of a friendly letter. As appropriate, review the personal letter format (with return address, salutation, etc.) or write a model letter on the chalkboard; for example:

Dear Mom and Dad, (or Aunt Thelma, or Bill,)

Look! I've learned how to write in cursive. What do you think of my writing? I still have to print my work papers in school.

Love,

Each letter should contain a question to generate a response. If a model like this is used, children should be encouraged to add at least one original sentence to the letter.

Give pupils a chance to compose a draft copy of the letter. Review their drafts, checking on letter formation as well as on spelling, sentence structure, and mechanics. Have pupils copy corrected drafts and bring or mail the letters to the people for whom they are intended.

It is important that all letters be sent, as this activity is designed to put the practice of handwriting into a truly communicative context.

Evaluation Criteria: Pupils' completed letters.

Extension and Integration:

WRITING: To the extent that children have the opportunity to incorporate their own sentences into their letters, sentence writing is a focus of the activity.

LANGUAGE: After pupils have written a first draft, review with the class the conventions of capitalization and punctuation normally practiced in a letter.

SPEAKING: As a follow-up, have pupils share the responses—either spoken or written—that they received from the adults to whom the letters were sent.

TONGUE TWISTERS

Skill Area: Language: Handwriting

Background: Practice coupled with purpose constitute the key ingredients of handwriting instruction. If students are encouraged to practice their handwriting for the expressed purpose of sharing final products with peers, legible handwriting will be assured. In the following activity, students are asked to practice writing tongue twisters which will be exchanged and read by other students.

Objective: The students will practice writing tongue twisters using proper letter formations and spacing between words.

Materials: Handwriting worksheets; tongue twisters (examples provided).

Activity: Prepare a handwriting worksheet.

for each of the following tongue twisters:

> toyboat
> three tree twigs
> Greek Grapes
> black bug's blood

Make five or six copies of each worksheet.

Say the popular tongue twister, "Peter Piper Picked a Peck of Pickled Peppers," for the class and explain the term "tongue twister."

Divide the class into groups of five or six students. Distribute a different handwriting worksheet to each group. Have students in each group practice writing their tongue twister three times, emphasizing the importance of using their best handwriting because someone in another group is going to read their handwriting. Some children may benefit from tracing the printed tongue twister before writing their own.

When the students have completed the worksheet, direct them to examine their handwriting, making sure that their letters are properly formed and spaces have been left between words (give them time to make corrections).

Have groups exchange their worksheets with each other. Have one group read its tongue twister three times to the rest of the class, reading it slowly the first time and quickly the second time. Have the whole class try to say it. Move on to the next group then.

Ask students to comment on the handwriting of the papers they are reading. Discuss the importance of good handwriting.

Evaluation Criteria: Students' ability to form letters properly and to space between words while writing tongue twisters.

Extension and Integration:

LISTENING/SPEAKING: An excellent resource for tongue twisters is Brown, Maria. *Peter Piper's Alphabet.* New York: Scribner's, 1959. Delight children with these various tongue twisters and encourage them to try a few.

WRITING: Have students analyze the alliterative pattern (same initial consonant in Peter Piper Picked a Peck of Pickled Peppers) contained in many tongue twisters and create their own tongue twisters using the same pattern.

READING: Tongue twisters are a fun way for students to practice their decoding skills, for example, students can focus on decoding the consonant blend, *pl,* in the following tongue twister: Pam placed plump plums on the plow.

TWENTY-SIX LETTERS IN A SENTENCE

Skill Area: Language
Handwriting

Background: Many students find handwriting practice a largely uninteresting enterprise. Yet, practice is important to mastery. The trick in planning practice activities is to inject something besides practice per se into the exercise.

Objective: Students will practice handwriting, while at the same time think of sentences that contain all twenty-six letters of the alphabet.

Materials: None.

Activity: Write the following sentence on the chalkboard or on an overhead transparency and have the class read it aloud:

The quick brown fox jumps over the lazy dog.

Explain that the sentence, while it doesn't make a great deal of sense, is frequently used for handwriting practice because the sentence contains all twenty-six letters of the alphabet.
Some suggested samples:

William fixed the broken zipper on his green jacket very quickly.
Five angry zoo animals just quenched their thirst anxiously by the dark water pool.

Divide the class into small groups to write similar sentences. Give students enough time to work on this activity: it's not as easy as it first seems! After groups have produced sentences, have students practice handwriting by copying these sentences.

Evaluation Criteria: Students' ability to produce these sentences and copy them with good handwriting.

Extension and Integration:

LISTENING: To help students increase auditory memory, orally read sentences that groups construct and have students repeat them.

READING: Use the sentences that groups dictate for practice in oral reading or choral reading with the class.

SPEAKING: Students can act out or pantomime sentences that individual children or groups create.

GRAPHOLOGY

Skill Area: Language
Handwriting

Background: Legibility is the goal of handwriting instruction, and to achieve it students must attend to four key elements: shape, size, slant, and space. Increasing student awareness about these elements is important and can best be achieved by encouraging students to evaluate the legibility of their own handwriting. In the following activity, graphology, the study of handwriting is used as an entertaining way of introducing students to the legibility factors. Students are then asked to evaluate their handwriting according to these factors.

Objective: Given a series of questions, students will analyze their handwriting for four factors: shape, size, slant, and space.

Materials: Graphology chart (example provided); worksheet.

Activity: Write a message, six to eight lines in length, on the board and ask students to copy it. Have students compare their handwriting with neighbors and ask them to describe some similarities/differences that they see, such as, "He writes bigger than I do" or "My handwriting tilts backwards." List responses on the board.

Ask students if they have ever heard of graphology. Discuss responses and explain that graphology is the study of handwriting. Explain that graphologists—handwriting experts—believe that you can tell a lot about an individual's personality by analyzing his or her handwriting. Suggest that it would be fun to have them try and analyze their handwriting to find out more about their personality.

Present the following chart to the students. (Note: Graphologists assign a wide range of personality characteristics to each handwriting element. For example, large handwriting may indicate a personality that is fun-loving, adventurous, and friendly or it may also indicate that a person is conceited and wants to be the center of attraction. For our purposes, however, the chart below identifies only a few characteristics for each element, and all are positive personality characteristics. (The purpose of the activity is to have students think about elements that lead to legible handwriting, not to psychoanalyze themselves.)

Introduce the first handwriting element (slant) on the chart to students. Ask students to analyze their writing samples and decide if their slant is forward, vertical, or backward. Explain the personality characteristics associated with each slant. Have students, at the bottom of their writing sample, write the slant that characterizes their writing and the personality characteristic that they think they possess, for example: forward slant—friendly.

Slant

Forward: a forward slant may reveal that the person is friendly and outgoing. Here's an example of a forward slant:

forward slant

Vertical: a vertical or straight up and down slant may show that a person is dependable and hard-working. Here is example:

vertical slant

Backward: a backward slant may reveal that a person is independent (likes to do things by him or herself) and is a logical. Here is an example:

backward slant

Size

Large size handwriting: This may indicate that a person is adventurous and generous. An example:

large size handwriting

Small handwriting: This may show that a person is a very careful worker and accepting of other people. An example:

small handwriting

Shape

Round letters: People who use round shapes are usually easy going and patient An example:

round letters

Pointed letters: People who make pointy letter shapes are often ambitious (want to get ahead) and persistent (stick with something until it is done). An example:

pointed letters

Spacing

Large spaces: People who leave large spaces between their words may be open-minded and friendly. An example:

large spaces between their words

Small spaces: People who leave only small spaces between their words may be careful workers and thrifty with their money. An example:

small spaces between their words

Repeat this procedure with the remaining handwriting elements. Have students react to their brief personality profiles.

Emphasize that while no two people have the same personality or handwriting style, it is important that all handwriting be legible because we write to communicate a message and if it can't be read, we aren't communicating.

Pass out the following worksheet and ask students to reexamine the same four elements of their handwriting:

	YES	NO	SOMETIMES
SLANT			
Does your writing slant too far to the right?	——	——	——————
Does your writing slant too far to the left?	——	——	——————
Do some letters in a word slant one way and other letters slant another way?	——	——	——————
Do you need to work on your slant?	——	——	——————
LETTER SHAPE			
Do you have trouble making any letters?	——	——	——————
Which ones?			
Do you need to work on your letter shapes?	——	——	——————
Do your e's look like i's without the dot?	——	——	——————
Do your i's look like e's with a dot?	——	——	——————
Do your a's look like u's?	——	——	——————
Do your d's look like cl?	——	——	——————
Do you cross your t's?	——	——	——————
SIZE			
Does your writing look too big?	——	——	——————
Does your writing look too small?	——	——	——————

Do some words look big and some words look small?	____	____	_____
Do you need to change your size?	____	____	_____
SPACE			
Do you write your letters too close together?	____	____	_____
Do you write your letters too far apart?	____	____	_____
Do you leave too much space between your words?	____	____	_____
Do you leave too little space between your words?	____	____	_____
Do you need to work on spacing?	____	____	_____

If possible conference individually with students about their handwriting evaluations; have them explain to you what areas they need to concentrate on as they write. You might ask the student to write a sentence for you so that you can determine what may be causing the problem; make suggestions for correcting the problem if possible.

Evaluation Criterion: Students' ability to analyze the legibility of their handwriting by responding to questions.

Extension and Integration:

READING: Encourage students to research the various roles that graphologists have in our society (such as detecting forgeries for police; analyzing personalities of prospective job candidates for businesses, etc.).

HANDWRITING: Let students receive feedback from their peers about the legibility of their handwriting. Students can exchange writing samples and evaluate each others' handwriting using the above checklist.

LISTENING: Use any of the following films or filmstrips to reinforce classroom instruction:

Films:

History of Writing. Chicago: Encyclopedia Britannica Films.
Improve Your Handwriting. Chicago: Coronet Films.
Writing Different Kinds of Letters. Chicago: Coronet Films.

Filmstrips:

Improve Your Handwriting. New York: Young American Films, Inc.
Step by Step Handwriting. Chicago: Society for Visual Education.

PUNCTUATION GAMES

Skill Area: Language
Punctuation

Background: Providing students with a variety of punctuation activities will enhance their punctuation power. The following games challenge students to apply their punctuation knowledge.

Objective: Given sentences with punctuation deleted, the students will select the correct punctuation mark.

Materials: A worksheet with four punctuation marks (example provided); index cards containing sentences and punctuation marks.

Activity: Prepare a worksheet that contains four punctuation marks.

Have students cut out each punctuation shape. Review the purpose of each punctuation mark.

Write a group of sentences with punctuation deleted on the board; for example:

Who likes peanut butter and pickle sandwiches ☐

Oh, no, I just dropped my ice cream cone ☐

Two popular fruits are apples and oranges ☐

Look at that hot fudge sundae ☐

Ted's favorite desserts are doughnuts ☐ apple pie ☐ ice cream ☐ and jello ☐

Instruct students to listen as you read the first sentence from the board and to hold up the punctuation mark that belongs in the box as quickly as possible. Have students explain their choice. Repeat procedure with the remaining sentences.

Students can then divide into smaller groups and play Concentrate and Punctuate (a variation of concentration). Pass out two sets of cards to each group. The set A cards contain sentences with punctuation deleted (boxes to indicate where punctuation belongs); the set B cards contain corresponding punctuation marks. Students can arrange the cards as follows:

Set A   Set B

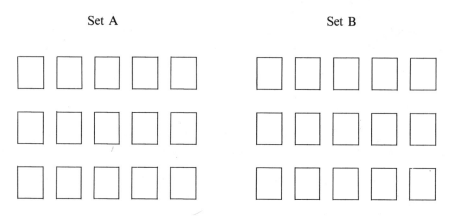

One student turns over a card from Set A and one card from Set B. If the punctuation mark fits the sentence, the student has a match and keeps both cards. If the punctuation mark doesn't fit the sentence, the student returns each card to its place and another player takes a turn. The student with the most matches wins.

Evaluation Criterion: Students' ability to select correct punctuation marks.

Extension and Integration:

WRITING: Have students apply punctuation knowledge by correctly punctuating a notice being sent home to their parents. The notice can then be rewritten, using best handwriting, and taken home to parents.

SPEAKING: Hold up a punctuation mark (on a large card) and ask students to create sentences that correspond to the punctuation mark.

READING: Reading with expression presumes an understanding of punctuation. To illustrate this point to students, write the following sentences on the board:

A storm is coming.
A storm is coming?
A storm is coming!

Have students read each sentence with appropriate intonation. Discuss differences.

Plays also provide students with an excellent opportunity to read with expression.

PUNCTUATE THE ROOM

Skill Area: Language
Punctuation

Background: In teaching punctuation, we typically introduce students to the rules associated with each punctuation mark and ask them to apply these rules in their writing. However, the realization that students may not really understand the function of punctuation becomes evident with that first set of over- or under-punctuated papers. One solution to this problem is to have the students themselves generate the generalizations that govern punctuation and apply them accordingly.

Objective: The students will correctly punctuate a wall message.

Materials: Index cards; headlines/titles from magazines; construction paper.

Activity: Write various punctuation marks (period, comma, question mark, exclamation point, quotation marks) appropriate to students' grade level on index cards, one mark per card.

Cut out magazine headings/titles that illustrate various uses of each punctuation mark. For example, for a period, the following items were selected:

a. an ad: Come to bermuda this winter. (after a statement)
b. a headline: The New Ms. U.S.A. (after abbreviations)
c. a listing:
    1. Poultry
    2. Lamb (after numbers in a list)

Tape the index card | Period | to the board and the three pieces of representative material. Tell students that punctuation marks have a number of jobs to do. Ask them to look at the examples on the board and figure out the three jobs of a period. Discuss responses.

Divide the class into groups; hand each group an index card with a different punctuation mark and representative materials. Have students in each group examine the materials and write down the jobs of their punctuation mark. Groups can then share results. Encourage each group to make a punctuation mobile for their punctuation mark; mobiles can be hung around the room for future reference.

Have students apply their punctuation knowledge by punctuating a message attached to a classroom wall. The message (with all punctuation deleted) can be written on consecutive pieces of construction paper and taped to one wall of the classroom (within children's reaching distance). A series of punctuation marks (in triangular shapes) are taped to the wall, just below the message.

> Great news   On Dec   4   our
>
> new classroom pet   a hamster
>
> will arrive   What do you think
>
> we should name him   If you
>
> have a suggestion   write it
>
> down and put it in the box
>
> △ △ △ △ △ △ △ △ △ △

The activity can be organized in different ways:

1. Students can copy down the message and punctuate accordingly. Ask students to come up and place the punctuation marks on the wall chart.
2. Divide the class into two teams. Hold up a punctuation mark; the first person to raise his or her hand and accurately place the punctuation mark on the wall chart wins a point for his or her team.
3. Encourage students to punctuate the wall chart independently during free time.

Change the message frequently so as to maximize the novelty effect.

Evaluation Criterion: Students' ability to punctuate sentences correctly.

Extension and Integration:

LANGUAGE: Write the same message on four charts with all punctuation deleted. Divide the class into four groups. The first group to punctuate the message correctly, wins.

WRITING: Have students create messages for the wall by first writing their drafts with appropriate punctuation on scrap paper and then transferring it to the wall with punctuation deleted.

WRITING: Writing a letter on the wall using above procedures will provide students with an excellent visual model of a letter's format and punctuation. Students can write their own letters, using the model as a guide.

CAN I QUOTE YOU ON THAT?

Skill Area: Language
Punctuation

Background: The confusion experienced by many students learning to use quotation marks is typified by a fourth grader who wrote in his football story, Get out there and win, ''hollered the Coach.'' Students need clarification as to what words are punctuated with quotation marks and why. The following activity provides students with an opportunity to transform the dialogue of a comic strip into a story containing direct quotes.

Objective: The students will design a comic strip for an unfinished story and then transform the comic strip into a story containing direct quotations.

Materials: Comic strip (example provided); construction paper.

Activity: Write the following sentences on the board:

a. Ted said that he likes peanut butter and jelly sandwiches.　　Ted said, ''I want to get my car painted.''

b. Ted said that he wants to get his car painted.　　Ted said, ''I would like to buy a boat and a motorcycle.''

c. Ted said that he would like to buy a boat and a motorcycle.　　Ted said, ''I like peanut butter and jelly sandwiches.''

Have the students read the sentences and match those that have the same meaning. Ask the students what the difference is between the A sentences and the B sentences. Discuss what quotation marks are and how they are used to set off the exact words of the speaker. Point out that the first word of the quotation is capitalized and that the punctuation mark at the end of quotation comes before the final quotation mark.

Prepare a short unfinished comic strip, similar to the following example and place it on the overhead projector.

Read the comic strip and ask students to repeat the first thing that Ted said to Louie. As students respond, write the words and punctuate accordingly:

"Wow, Ted, where did you get that minibike?" asked Louie.

Explain the quotation marks and their purpose. Have the class as a group translate the comic strip into a story containing direct quotes. The finished product will be similar to this:

Louie was on his way to the ball park when he saw Ted with his new minibike.
"Wow, Ted, where did you get that minibike?" asked Louie.
"I just got it for my birthday," said Ted.
Louie asked, "How fast does it go?"
"About 30 miles per hour," replied Ted.
Ted started the engine.
"Hey Louie, watch me ride it down the road," shouted Ted.

During the creation of this first draft, continually ask what words are being spoken by the character and where the quotation marks go. Attention may also be given to other punctuation marks.

Pass out construction paper and have students fold their paper into six boxes. Remind them that the comic strip about Ted and Louie is unfinished. Ask them to illustrate the remainder of the comic strip. Students can then transform their comic strips into story endings, complete with direct quotations, properly punctuated.

Evaluation Criterion: Students' ability to correctly punctuate direct quotations.

Extension and Integration:

LANGUAGE: Students can generalize about other punctuation marks, (commas, question marks, etc.) found in quotations by examining sentences illustrating a specific punctuation mark and deciding on the rule.

WRITING: Have students select comic strips from the Sunday funnies and transform them into stories containing direct quotes.

READING: Have students bring in newspaper articles that contain direct quotes. Discuss why newspaper reporters include direct quotes in their stories.

BATTING A THOUSAND

Skill Area: Language
Punctuation

Background: Ongoing assessment is the key to effective instruction. The following activity can be used to informally assess students' mastery of punctuation and identify students in further need of instruction.

Objective: Given worksheets of increasing difficulty, the students will punctuate the sentences correctly.

Materials: Batter's Cage Worksheets (example provided).

Activity: Write the following lists on the board or on a chart:

PUNCTUATION MARK	PLACE
	at the end of a question
period	around the words of a speaker
comma	after an abbreviation
question mark	at the end of an exciting sentence
exclamation point	between things in a series
quotation marks	after the day in a date
	at the end of a sentence

Have students match up the punctuation marks and places. Clarify any confusion with examples.

Prepare four punctuation worksheets of increasing difficulty in the format of batters' cages. The first and easiest worksheet, titled *Little League,* requires students to fill in ending punctuation marks (periods, question mark, exclamation points):

Little League

1. Who has made the most homeruns in baseball ☐
2. The umpire calls the balls and the strikes ☐
3. Which team won the 1982 World Series ☐
4. How many hot dogs did you eat at the game ☐
5. The pitcher is walking to the mound ☐
6. The fans are going wild ☐
7. Baseball is a popular sport ☐
8. What a great game ☐

Design the three remaining worksheets in the same fashion.

The second worksheet can be titled *Minor League,* requiring commas as well as ending punctuation. The third worksheet can be titled *Major League,* requiring quotation marks in addition to commas and ending punctuation. The last worksheet, titled *National League,* can assess all of the previous punctuation marks.

Introduce these worksheets to students by asking if anyone has ever been to the Batter's Cage at an amusement park. Have students explain varying degrees of difficulty associated with each cage; introduce terms: Little League, Minor League, Major League, and National League.

Tape the four worksheets to the board. Point to the first batter's cage, titled *Little League*. Tell students this is the easiest cage in which to score a hit because they only have to punctuate the end of each statement with a period, question mark, or exclamation point.

Assign two students to the role of umpire; their job is to correct students' papers. Upon completing the first worksheet, students are to bring their papers to one of the umpires. Students who punctuate six or more sentences correctly qualify for the next batter's cage. Students who do not score six hits can be given another chance to complete the worksheet.

Evaluation Criterion: Students' ability to punctuate correctly.

Extension and Integration:

PUNCTUATION: Allow students to score extra hits by correctly editing the punctuation of previously drafted stories.

PUNCTUATION: Students who move through each of the batter's cages successfully can qualify for the World Series Game. A baseball diamond can be drawn on the board and two teams formed. Students who punctuate accurately score hits for their team.

READING/WRITING: Students can test their baseball knowledge by answering questions raised in the worksheets. Responses must be correctly punctuated.

REFERENCES

ADELSON, LEONE. *Dandelions Don't Bite*. New York: Pantheon, 1972.

AKINS, W. R. *ESP—Your Psychic Powers and How To Test Them*. New York: Franklin Watts, 1980.

BERGER, MELVIN. *The Supernatural: From ESP to UFO's*. New York: John Day Co., 1970.

BERGER, TERRY. *A Friend Can Help*. Chicago: Raintree Editions, 1974.

BROWN, MARIA. *Peter Piper's Alphabet*. New York: Scribner's, 1959.

BROWN, MARION and CANE, RUTH. *The Silent Storm*. Nashville, Tenn.: Abingdon, 1963.

BYARS, BETSY. *The Summer of the Swans*. New York: Viking, 1970.

CANTY, MARY. *The Green Gate*. New York: D. McKay, 1965.

CHRISTOPHER, MATTHEW. *Long Shot for Paul*. Boston: Little, Brown, 1966.

DAVIDSON, JESSICA. *Is that Mother in the Bottle?* New York: Franklin Watts, 1972.

De ANGELI, MARGUERITE. *The Door in the Wall*. New York: Doubleday, 1972.

DITZEL, PAUL. *Fire Engines, Firefighter*. New York: Crown, 1974.

EBON, MARTIN. *Test Your ESP*. New York: Thomas Y. Crowell, 1970.

EDELSON, EDWARD. *The Book of Prophecy*. New York: Doubleday, 1974.

FUNK, CHARLES. *Heavens to Betsy and Other Curious Sayings*. New York: Harper & Row, Pub., 1955.

FREDERICK, GUY. *101 Best Magic Tricks*. New York: Bell Publishing Co., 1966.

GAEDDERT, LORI ANN. *Noisy Nancy Noms and Nick*. New York: Doubleday, 1970.

GELLER, URI. *My Story*. New York: Praeger, 1975.

GEORGE, JEAN. *Julia of the Wolves*. New York: Harper & Row, 1972.

GLICKMAN, PAUL. *Magic Tricks*. New York: Franklin Watts, 1980.

GOFFSTEIN, M. B. *Two Piano Tuners*. New York: Farrar, Straus & Giroux, 1970.

GREALISH, MARY JANE and GREALISH, CHARLES. *Amy Maura*. New York: Human Policy Press, 1975.

KEATS, EZRA. *Apartment No. 3.* New York: Macmillan, 1971.

KEIFFER, ELIZABETH. "Overcoming the Odds." *Good Housekeeping,* March, 1976.

KONIGSBURG, E. L. *From the Mixed-Up Files of Mrs. Basil E. Frankweiler.* New York: Random House/Innovation Press, 1967.

KRENSKY, JOSEPH and LINFIELD, JORDAN. *The Bad Speller's Dictionary.* New York: Random House/Innovation Press, 1967.

LINDGREN, ASTRID. *Pippi Longstocking.* New York: Viking, 1950.

LITTLE, JEAN. *Mine for Keeps.* Boston: Little, Brown, 1962.

LUIS, EARLENE and MILLAR, BARBARA. *Listen Lissa.* New York: Dodd, Mead, 1968.

McCASLIN, NELLIE. *Creative Drama in the Classroom.* New York: Longman Inc., 1980.

McCORMACK, JoANN. *The Story of our Language.* Columbus, Ohio: Chas. E. Merrill, 1967.

MOFFETT, JAMES and WAGNER, BETTY JANE. *Student-Centered Language Arts and Reading, K-13.* Boston: Houghton Mifflin Co., 1976.

NAYLOR, PHILLIS. *Getting Along with Your Friends.* Nashville, Tenn.: Abingdon, 1980.

NESS, EVALINE. *Sam, Bangs and Moonshine.* New York: Holt, Rinehart & Winston, 1966.

PEARSON, P. DAVID and JOHNSON DALE. *Teaching Reading Comprehension.* New York: Holt, Rinehart & Winston, 1972.

PETERSON, JEANNE W. *I Have a Sister, My Sister is Deaf.* New York: Harper & Row, Pub., 1977.

RHINE, LOUISA. *Mind over Matter.* New York: Macmillan, 1970.

SAGE, MICHAEL. *If You Talked to a Boar.* Philadelphia: Lippincott, 1960.

SAVAGE, JOHN F. *Effective Communication: Language Arts Instruction in the Elementary School.* Chicago: Science Research Associates, 1977.

SENDAK, MAURICE. *Where the Wild Things Are.* New York: Harper & Row, Pub., 1963.

SILVERSTEIN, SHEL. *The Giving Tree.* New York: Harper & Row, Pub., 1964.

STAUFFER, RUSSEL. *Directing the Reading-Thinking Process.* New York: Harper & Row, Pub., 1975.

STEINER, CHARLOTTE. *A Friend is Amie.* New York: Knopf, 1956.

STODDARD, EDWARD. *The First Book of Magic.* New York: Franklin Watts, 1977.

THORNE, IIAN. *Dracula.* New York: Crestwood House, Inc., 1977.

VAN GELDER, ROSALIND. *Monkeys have Tails.* New York: D. McKay, 1961.

WAHL, JAN. *A Wolf of My Own.* New York: Macmillan, 1970.

WHITE, E. B. *Charlotte's Web.* New York: Harper & Row, Pub., 1952.

WHITE, MARY. *Twin Words.* New York: Abingdon Press, 1961.

WOLF, BERNARD. *Connie's New Eyes.* New York: Lippincott, 1976.

WOLF, BERNARD. *Anna's Silent World.* New York: Lippincott, 1977.

ZOLOTOW, CHARLOTTE. *The New Friend.* New York: Abelard-Schuman, 1968.

ZOLOTOW, CHARLOTTE. *William's Doll.* New York: Harper & Row, Pub., 1972.

ZOLOTOW, CHARLOTTE. *Janey.* New York: Harper & Row, Pub., 1973.

INDEX

LB1576 .J38 1983   CU-Main

Jenkins, Carol A., /Activities for integrating the

3 9371 00005 9527

LB
1576   Jenkins, Carol A.
J38   Activities for integrating
1983   The Language Arts

LB
1576
J38   Jenkins, Carol A.
1983   Activities for integrating
         the Language Arts

DATE DUE	BORROWER'S NAME	ROOM NUMBER
JUN 1 '85	Ross Besel	
DEC 15 85	Corinne Hill	
MAY 1 '86	Jeanne Hill	EH 207
MAY 15 '86	Cheril A.	

CONCORDIA COLLEGE LIBRARY
2811 N. E. HOLMAN ST.
PORTLAND, OREGON 97211